THE ENCYCLOPEDIA
OF THE
WEIRD
AND
WONDERFUL

THE ENCYCLOPEDIA
OF THE
WEIRD
AND
WONDERFUL

MILO ROSSI

CURIOUS AND INCREDIBLE
FACTS THAT WILL
BLOW YOUR MIND

wellfleet
press

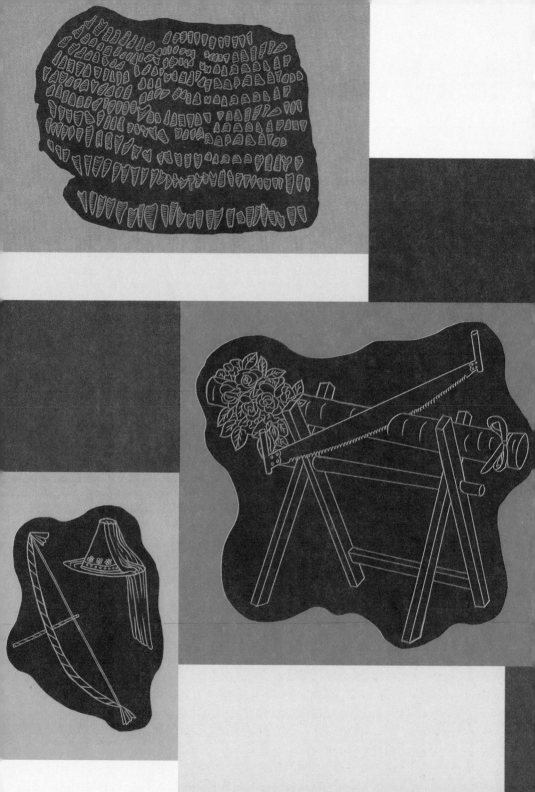

FOR MY MOTHER'S GIFT OF WORDS
AND MY FATHER'S SENSE OF PURPOSE

CONTENTS

INTRODUCTION

✦ ✳ ✦ ✴

We are all familiar with the phrase "history repeats itself," and while this is most frequently preceded by a sigh and a particularly dour outlook on the current political state, this saying is one that I believe has a much more profound meaning.

We tend to view our history as linear: a long string of technological innovations and historical events that brought us to the world we share today. While I would agree that historical events and advancements are, for the most part, a linear progression, the story of humanity itself is completely different. Our story is not a linear event, but a wheel—an ever-turning cycle as the most incredible species to walk the face of the planet continues to reinvent the world around us despite our most primal needs and frivolous desires remaining unchanged. You and I are the most recent entry in the book of humankind that has been written for far, far longer than many of us think.

Our species, *Homo sapiens*, has existed functionally as we do today for the last two hundred thousand years. For the entire duration of this time, our world has been home to people who were exactly like you and me. People who walked upright and carried their children on their backs when the youngster's little legs were too tired to press on. People who turned their faces toward the sky to laugh as they felt the first heavy drops of rain fall after a summer of drought and splashed in the puddles when the deluge subsided. People who felt the flames of love, the elation of laughter, and the sting of loss.

If you were to think of any point in history, your mind would likely jump to great events or the places where they occurred. Perhaps the Hittites would come to mind, who, sword in hand, ushered forth the beginning of the Iron Age. Perhaps your imagination would take you to the stabbing of Julius Caesar on the Senate floor, or to a bloodstained field where the crack of rifle fire and the courageous commands of Major General Meade echo as he led his troops to a decisive victory at the Battle of Gettysburg.

But have you ever wondered what it was like to be a mother during the Mesolithic period as the climate shifted, the seas rose, and wild game migrated? Or what types of dogs paced the wide streets and narrow forest paths of North America as their masters constructed some of the largest earthen works in the world? Or what meals were eaten by starlight under the old-growth forests of ancient Europe, how China accidentally invented standardized testing by refining their government, or what fashion trends shook the mining camps during the California Gold Rush?

With no one left from these times it can be hard to look back upon the people of the past and think of them as more than just a faceless horde. But it is these average people who *make* history. With an estimated 120 billion people having lived, breathed, and died on this spinning celestial rock, it is no small wonder that the names that withstand the test of time are those who accomplished great feats and not those who jumped a little too hard in a puddle and got soaked.

Yet there is something about these "simple" stories that puts a smile on our faces. Something so timeless about a shared human experience that enchants the imagination more than an index of great events in the back of a dusty textbook. You could read about the speculated life of the great Viking Ragnar Lothbrok and surely be captivated by the stories of this legendary hero. Yet no matter how great his achievements may be, there is something about the simple story of another Viking who once stood 10 feet (3 m) above sea level and felt the need to carve into a rock "I am very high up" that fascinates us in a much different (but equally powerful) way. While this Viking's name may be long lost to time, it is safe to say that his sense of humor is one that transcends nearly a thousand years of human development.

Despite the more mundane experiences frequently being left out of the history books, the evidence for it litters our world. While we cannot resurrect every tale in our history, there are countless that resonate as part of the cyclical human experience. For this reason, this book has been divided into chapters based around the stages of life. We will start at the very beginning (a very good place to start) with birth and early childhood. As we make our way through this human story we will learn about the meals we ate, love and sexuality, fashion statements, work and education, and, finally, the great equalizer—death—and the burial practices it has inspired. As we walk the cyclical human story, we will be covering all time periods—from prehistory (my specialty) to the turn of the last century—as well as geographic regions. All to emphasize that, no matter where (or when) we are from, we are all part of one ever-turning wheel of life.

From our crowning achievements to our simple pleasures, and everything in between, I sincerely hope that the stories within these pages will allow you to feel more in touch with those who walked this Earth before us and, perhaps, even yourself. Without further ado, my friends, welcome to The Encyclopedia of the Weird and Wonderful.

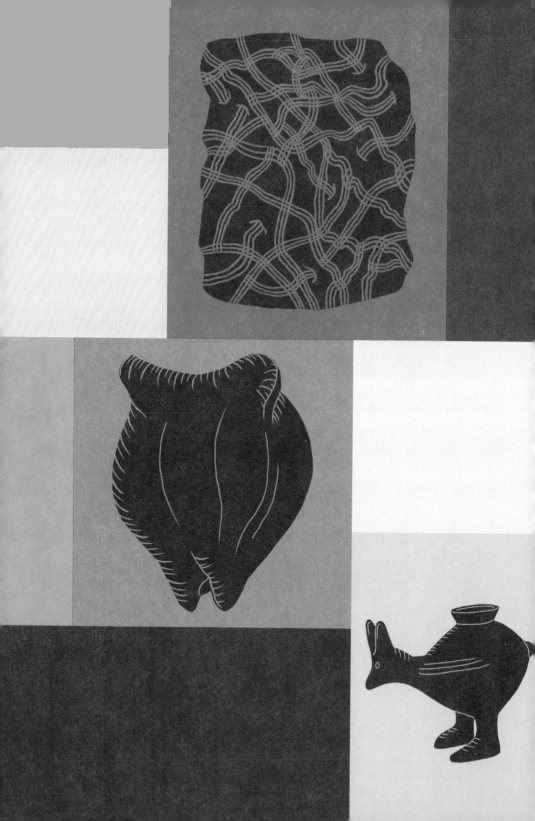

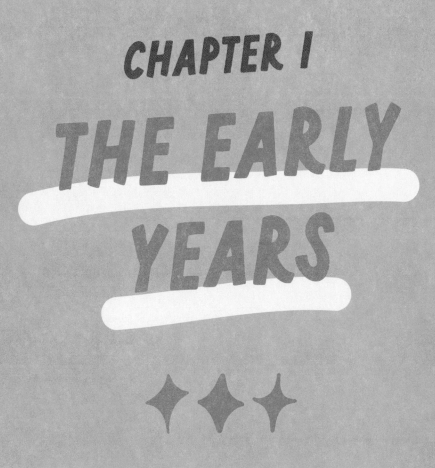

CHAPTER 1

THE EARLY YEARS

Everyone's childhood is different, but the threads of curiosity and development are the same for all. From searching the crumbling wood of a rotten log for pill bugs to delightfully smearing ketchup on the walls because you can, children have always been curious about the world and learning how it works through trial and error. So, as you reminisce about that favorite childhood story, remember that you are the most recent chapter in a ceaseless human tradition of childhood wonder and discovery.

THE WHITE SANDS PRINTS

A small, rounded stone sat half-buried in a powdery bed of white gypsum dust. While most would have strolled past this tiny lithic without a second glance, the boys who ambled up the shoreline had an eye for anything that could be thrown, swung, or otherwise set into abrupt motion. Sure enough, the youngest of the two ran ahead, whooping with excitement, to retrieve this tiny piece of entertainment potential from the mucky lakeshore. He turned to face the expanse of water in front of him and, carefully cradling the rock between his index finger and thumb, twisted his torso slowly back before unleashing the entirety of his six-year-old manpower. The rock whizzed out of his hand and glanced off the mirrored surface of the water. It bounced again, and again, then again once more before it caught an edge and disappeared with a splash. The boy watched the water with his dark eyes as the ripples spread before he let out a disgruntled huff and trotted up the dune toward his chaperone.

The youngster scrambled on all fours past the tufts of yucca and the cheerful yellow blossoms of green thread stalks. At the top of the dune he stopped abruptly next to his brother, who gazed down into the lush valley and let out a low sigh of awe. Below, a group of enormous beasts shambled their way to the swollen lakeshore through the ripples of a shifting sea of grass. Their coats were shaggy and dark, and wet gypsum from the valley floor had splashed and dried around their legs. Each slow and lumbering step required correction to ensure that the beast remained pointed in the right direction as its enormous feet slid on the slick substrate. The boys stood upright and gazed in wonder at the procession below.

Both knew that these lumbering creatures posed no threat to them, so long as they kept their distance. The youngest of the two looked down at the herd and jumped up and down, waving his hands in the air and hooting with excitement. Several juvenile sloths that had

RADIOCARBON DATING IN EXPOSURE TO WATER

A passion of mine is correcting archaeological misinformation, which is why I feel the need to insert a tidbit of knowledge here that hopefully you will find useful if you are ever confronted with someone who tries to tell you that radiocarbon dating (RCD) is impossible to do on samples that have been exposed to water. Considering that the seeds of our humble little pond weed are an example of wet-environment RCD, I think it would be a wonderful opportunity to lend some clarity to the topic.

So, does water affect the process of radiocarbon dating? Long story short: yes. But before you run off to tell your friends that this proves the Earth is only six thousand years old, allow me to explain. The effects that both freshwater and saltwater have on RCD are referred to as the freshwater reservoir effect and the saltwater reservoir effect respectively. These effects have been known about by scientists for decades, and as a result, scientists go into wet environments ready to account for the error that the environment caused. Think of it like this: if you are driving at 60 miles per hour (97 km/h) and a cop passes you going 60 in the other direction, your speed would be clocked at 120 miles per hour (193 km/h), the relative speed of both vehicles traveling toward one another. However, it would be foolish to say you are traveling at 120 miles per hour (193 km/h), because you aren't. The radar accounts for this discrepancy between perceived and actual speed and clocks you the correct 60 miles per hour. This analogy works well to explain how calibrating for a known error can eliminate it. In the case of conducting RCD for wet samples, scientists know how to calibrate their tools to negate the errors it would otherwise cause, and subsequently eliminate them.

been playing on the outskirts, much like this youngster, started then shambled their way back to the protective flanks of their herd. One of the largest of the beasts turned its head slowly to gaze at the two tiny, bipedal figures who stood high on the grassy ridge. It uttered a low bellowing *moooooo* and returned to its duty of keeping up the rear.

When did people first set foot in North America? Despite the perceived simplicity of this question, it is one of the most contested topics in archaeology. When pressed, many might suggest that this "peopling," as it is referred to, occurred around 15,000 years before present (YBP). This date is derived from evidence of Clovis culture scattered across the continent from the lush forests of what is now known as the Pacific Northwest to the shimmering grasslands of the Great Plains.

But on September 23, 2021, a paper entitled "Evidence of Humans in North America During the Last Glacial Maximum" was published discussing this pivotal discovery. Several sets of human footprints

YBP

Throughout this book you will see me use the shorthand YBP as a stand-in for "years before present." While dating schemes such as BCE and CE are known as relative dating (a date derived from its relation to an event), YBP is an absolute dating method—one where the age of something falls along a linear timeline from youngest to oldest.

were discovered pressed into the ancient substrate in the vast plain of the Tularosa Basin, in what is now the White Sands National Park in New Mexico, USA. These prints were perceived to have been of immense antiquity due to the layer in which they were found. To obtain the information needed to accurately date the prints, archaeologists and scientists had to rely on a proxy.

In this case, that proxy came in the form of a handful of grass seeds from the species *Ruppia cirrhosa*, more commonly known as spiral ditch grass. Since these seeds could be found pressed into the footprints on the white sands, it could be inferred through the law of superposition that they were likely deposited around the same time. This meant that by dating the seeds, one could also learn the date of the footprints.

The seeds were dated to around 23,000 YBP, nearly ten thousand years before Clovis culture would leave its mark on the face of this glacier-dominated continent. Needless to say, this discovery rocked the world of archaeology, proving that humans had a presence in North America nearly ten thousand years before the previous oldest evidence suggested.

The ancient bank of Lake Otero within the White Sands desert has yielded tracks of several different individuals over a several-thousand-year time span. Of these, many seem to belong to children and young adults, suggesting that teenagers may have been tasked with making treks and hunting due to, perhaps, their higher energy and enthusiasm levels. There are also tracks of a woman accompanied by a smaller set of tracks, presumably those of her child, that trace their way along the bank.

This oasis in the prairie would have been a hub of activity for the enormous beasts that roamed the continent in the last glacial maximum. Prints along the bank show that nearly twenty thousand

CLOVIS CULTURE

Clovis culture is the name given to what is currently the oldest recognized material culture in North America. This name has been applied to a series of lithic artifacts known as Clovis points, which gain their name from their initial discovery near Clovis, New Mexico. The points themselves consist of around ten thousand examples of biface spear points bearing a characteristic flute that would have allowed them to be attached to a wooden handle. In situ examples of Clovis points have shown that they were used extensively by the Paleo-Indigenous populations of North America for hunting Pleistocene megafauna, such as bison and the infamous mastodon.

Examples of these unique artifacts can be found across the entire United States, as well as some as far south as Mexico and as far north as Alaska! Amazingly, it is theorized that this culture and tradition rose and spread over a span of five hundred years, suggesting a high level of interconnectivity between the Paleo-Indigenous communities of Turtle Island (the term given by Indigenous Peoples to the landmass now known as North America). The age of these points, however, is hotly contested, with conservative estimates pointing to around 11,000 YBP and more liberal estimates placing them to around 15,000 or even 25,000 YBP in some places.

years ago someone tried their luck at stalking a lumbering ground sloth, suggested by the human footprints found alongside—and at times inside—the prints of one of these ancient Pleistocene herbivores. Though we have no indication whether this hunt was successful or not.

WRITING ON THE WALLS

When I was young, the sidewalk in front of my best friend's house was in the middle of being repaired and one of the best things that this activity allows for is the permanent marking of your childhood

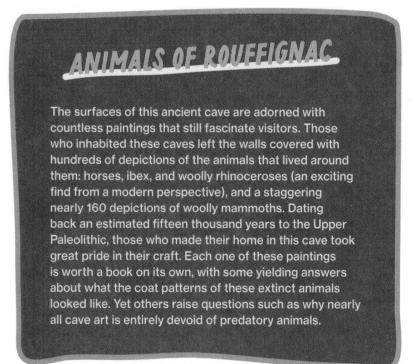

ANIMALS OF ROUFFIGNAC

The surfaces of this ancient cave are adorned with countless paintings that still fascinate visitors. Those who inhabited these caves left the walls covered with hundreds of depictions of the animals that lived around them: horses, ibex, and woolly rhinoceroses (an exciting find from a modern perspective), and a staggering nearly 160 depictions of woolly mammoths. Dating back an estimated fifteen thousand years to the Upper Paleolithic, those who made their home in this cave took great pride in their craft. Each one of these paintings is worth a book on its own, with some yielding answers about what the coat patterns of these extinct animals looked like. Yet others raise questions such as why nearly all cave art is entirely devoid of predatory animals.

turf by writing your initials in the wet cement. Unfortunately, I was not present that day, meaning only he was able to make his mark before the ticking clock of wet cement ran out. To this day, the tag "JHS 2011" sits in that slab of stone, a reminder of the boys who ruled that street twelve years ago. This is a tradition that children seem to have been drawn to for a veritable eternity. A wonderful ancient example comes to us from the walls and caverns of Rouffignac cave in France.

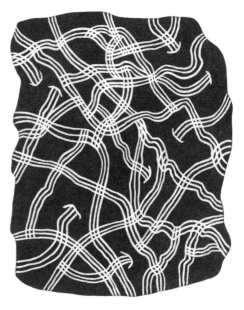

In the back of this cave system is a room whose walls are covered with small, thin, snaking lines. Each one was not painted but scraped into the soft clays that accumulate on the cave walls. These lines are known as "flutings" and are created by running one's fingers across this slippery surface. And it was by this very process that a group of children adorned the walls of Rouffignac cave some fifteen thousand years ago.

Fluting can act like a signature. The size of the fingers can be an accurate metric with which to determine the age of the artist, while the distance between each of the lines is a reliable way to tell the artists apart. Through these processes it was possible to identify that Rouffignac cave was once the home of around ten Paleolithic artists. It is believed that about half of them were between the ages of two and seven, determined by their personally unique signatures left in the soft clay. There was, however, one artist who seemed to be channeling the prolific nature of a Paleolithic Picasso. Believed to be a little girl, she was likely around the age of five at the time of her contribution to the cave flutings, but despite her age, it is her work that adorns more of the surface area of Rouffignac than anyone else.

While only about half of the flutings were made by children, all were accompanied by those of adults. It seems that this expression was a shared activity between children and their guardians, like teaching a child to do a craft or simply being there to encourage them as they figured it out for themselves. Many of these curling abstract patterns were found upward of 6 feet (1.8 m) off the ground. An impossible height for a child to reach, but no sweat with a boost from the strong arms of a loving adult. A timeless sign of parental love and encouragement from an ancient family that walked alongside mammoths and woolly rhinos.

WRITING ON THE WALLS . . . AGAIN??

You thought that was the only example of ancient children leaving their mark on the wet cement of history? Well, think again, bucko, because I've got another one for you. While the fifteen-thousand-year-old flutings in Rouffignac cave are of extreme antiquity, there is one discovery that dates back much, much, further.

Among the vast plains and jagged ridges of the Himalayan Plateau, archaeologists stumbled upon handprints that date back a staggering two hundred thousand years. Now solidified in limestone, these ancient markings were left behind by the hands and feet of children. For any readers who are well versed in the current concepts of human migration out of Africa, you may recognize this date as being nearly one hundred thousand years older than the hypothesized date that our H. sapiens ancestors set foot in a brave new world. Which means you understand correctly that these handprints were not left by our species. These prints are of such immense antiquity that it is currently hypothesized they were left by our elusive and mysterious ancestor, the Denisovans.

THE DENISOVANS

Who were the Denisovans? Great question! I have no idea. At the time of writing, our knowledge of Denisovans is wildly incomplete. It is currently based off a handful of teeth and bone fragments from Denisova Cave in Russia, Baishiya Cave in China, and Tam Ngu Hao 2 Cave in Laos. There is also the Dragon Man skull from China, which is hypothesized to be of Denisovan origin, although this has not been confirmed.

We do know, thanks to genetic analysis, that Denisovans branched off the line from modern humans a little more than a million years ago, which is earlier than the divergence of Neanderthals by about two hundred thousand years. Genetic analysis has also revealed that Denisovans share a little bit of their DNA with a human ancestor whose remains have yet to be discovered.

In fact, we know so little about them at this given moment that they don't even have a scientific name! They are currently classed under the genus *Homo*, but they have yet to be assigned a species. Current propositions include *H. altaiensis* and, of course, *H. denisova*.

I pray that someday this book falls into the hands of someone in 2030 or 2050 or beyond and they are able to look at this, chuckle, and think, "I can't believe how far our understanding has come." Well, my dear future reader, I can, and I am thrilled to hear it has.

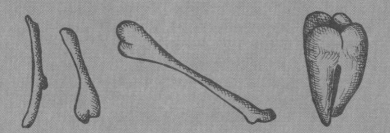

For much of the time that humans have known about our ancient ancestors they have been stereotyped in myriad unflattering ways, such as knuckle draggers and unsophisticated brutes. It seems as though our extinct hominid ancestors perpetually get a bad rep. This is a misconception that I am keen to disperse in any way I can, and it is stories like this that work to achieve that end. Our ancestors were, in the grand scheme of things, not all that different from you and me. Looking at these tiny handprints draws into our minds the excited and curious little ones who left them nearly a quarter of a million years ago.

THE LITTLE BEAR

Rattles are a versatile creation, producing a range of sounds and applications depending on their construction and intended usage. In the contemporary age, rattles are used as percussive musical instruments and, as one would guess, entertainment for curious babies. While modern rattles vary in usage, scope, and composition, the tradition of creating these simple yet satisfying instruments is far from new. Within their long history, one rattle stands out for its unique appearance.

In 2016, a four-thousand-year-old rattle was found in a settlement in the Novosibirsk region of what is now Russia. The artifact dates to the Bronze Age, nearly 4,000 YBP. Although the settlement contained examples of bronze metalworking, this artifact was made from expertly crafted and fired clay. The small spherical toy was created by encasing small stones within a clay hollow, and the clay was then fired to turn it rock solid, trapping the percussive stones inside.

What is most interesting is that the artist who set about making this rattle thousands of years ago took the time to decorate the outside of the clay to resemble the head of a bear cub. Even now, after all this time, the mouth, eyes, and face shape are still visible. These are all clear signs that the person who sculpted this little instrument gave it great care and could suggest that it was given to a child as a form of both visual and audible entertainment. There is even speculation that the tiny artifact still bears an ancient signature from the craftsman who made it.

It is humbling to look into the face of this fragile vessel and, as you hear the sound it still makes, know that the last person to hear that sound was someone's "little bear."

BABY BOTTLES

Imagine . . . you are in your local department store. Almost inevitably you will catch a glimpse at the baby shoes, if just to think: "Nothing should be allowed to have feet that tiny." Then, if you were to round the corner, you would surely be met with myriad baby bottles. What you won't be surprised to know, given this book, is that baby bottles are far from a new invention.

The presence of clay spout-bearing vessels as infant grave goods is something that dates back nearly seven thousand years in Europe. For many years, however, it was not confirmed what the use of these vessels was. This Neolithic pottery was assumed to be intended for use as a baby bottle or for feeding those who were bedridden, but there was no concrete evidence to support this until more recently.

The discovery of a handful of these wonderful vessels hailing from modern-day Bavaria yielded some insight into the matter. In a paper published in 2019, several of these bottles were analyzed in hopes of learning more about their potential contents. Despite their antiquity, these Bronze Age vessels still contained the residue of the substances they had contained nearly three thousand years ago. Sure enough, these vessels had once contained the milk of ruminants.

By having dairy animals, a supply of fresh milk would be ensured. The presence of baby bottles eliminates the necessity of a lactating mother to ensure an infant's survival; if a mother could not be present, a male or a non-lactating woman could be equally capable of caring for the child. This indicates not only that the world was trending toward an agricultural society and the beginnings of humans becoming dairy tolerant, but also the communal approach that this ancient group had toward raising children. By simply having a bottle, the job of raising a child—the oldest and most honorable job one can undertake—was something in which everyone could participate.

As the final icing on this cake, the bottles themselves have been found in countless shapes, from simple spheres with spouts to depictions of goats and sheep and abstract four-legged animals with heads and ears and legs. These delightful adornments are functionally useless. But despite all that, early humans still chose to make them like this. Why? Simply to make a baby smile. So when you walk past the baby bottles, remember that thousands of years ago someone held up a miniature vessel with four little legs and a tiny goat head by firelight and thought to themselves, "Oh yeah. My kid's gonna love this."

VROOM VROOM

Miniature models of various real-world items are a staple of early childhood entertainment. Children love to process the complexities of the world around them from the comfort of their own hands. Matchbox cars make banked turns as they zip around the living room, and families of dolls are subjected to the monotony and ceaseless drama of a child's interpretation of adult life.

I DAIRYOU TO DRINK THAT

The development of humankind to be able to digest lactose is a recent adaptation. You have likely been told by someone in a state of disgusted animation that "We are the only animal that drinks another animal's milk!!" This is a compelling moral argument that can be countered through the presence of a single Oreo cookie.

Milk contains a sugar called lactose, which gives it its sweetness as well as its nutritional value. While breastfeeding, humans will create lactase, which is dairy kryptonite that helps break down the lactose, making it usable for the body it finds itself in. Typically, the production of lactase stops as the drinker transitions to more adult beverages like water or an ice-cold Pabst Blue Ribbon.

About ten thousand years ago, humanity began to experiment with milk drinking in different parts of the world, from Africa to Europe. For whatever reason, people couldn't get enough of the stuff. But with hundreds of thousands of years of evolution telling our bodies to stop drinking it, we needed to overhaul our own system.

Slowly, humanity began to evolve the ability to produce lactase after early childhood and to consume a plethora of dairy products from milk to cheese, and even to Kraft singles. However, since it is such a recent adaptation in the grand scheme of human genetics and evolution, there is a 65 percent chance that you, reading this, have a reduced ability to digest lactose and a 15 percent chance of being fully lactose intolerant. Weird or not, the innate human desire to drink other animals' breast milk was so strong that it altered the course of our evolution.

"TOLIMA FIGHTER JETS"

I am absolutely fascinated by pseudoarchaeology and this is a perfect spot to insert an interesting story. The small, wheeled Mesoamerican toys are just one small piece of the "statuesque" material culture. From the Tolima region of what is now Colombia comes a collection of figurines made of solid gold that have been sensationally referred to as the "Tolima Fighter Jets."

This unfortunate and erroneous name comes from the fact that fictitious and pseudo-historical media, such as the hit television show *Ancient Aliens*, have tried to peddle these discoveries as proof that ancient Mesoamericans knew what fighter jets were and had contact with extraterrestrial beings. The evidence for this? Some of them sort of resemble an airplane. Comedically, *Ancient Aliens* attempted to prove their theory by building a flying replica of one of the models, removing things that decreased its aerodynamic qualities and adding little details like an engine, prop, landing gear, and articulated fins. Truly a laughable excuse for experimental archaeology.

As you won't be surprised to learn, these figurines are not fighter jets. In fact, they make up only a small portion of the Tolima Gold Figures. The rest include birds, lizards, and insects, each showing artistic interpretation and cultural flair. A difficult concept to grasp by those who ceaselessly hunt for evidence of extraterrestrials in our ancient past.

One ancient example of this tradition was discovered by Claude-Joseph Désiré Charnay in the late 1800s and miniature models have been continually found in places like the Tula archaeological site in central Mexico. These Mesoamerican discoveries consisted of several small animal figurines, which stumped archaeologists. It wasn't until the 1940s, when excavations were underway at the Tres Zapotes site in Veracruz, Mexico, that more of these unusual little critters were discovered.

To date, hundreds of these small figurines have been found scattered across the remains of classical (300–900 CE) and early post-classical Mesoamerican civilization. The subjects of these wonderful motifs range from dogs and deer to jaguars, alligators, and even armadillos. One of the most interesting pieces of these ancient toys is that many were found with wheels affixed to their tiny clay feet, allowing them, theoretically, to roll across the ground.

It is still unclear whether these statues were intended for children's play, as some are highly intricate and show a great deal of fragile craftsmanship, while others show signs of having been cast, allowing for some sort of mass production. While the jury may still be out on intended use, it is very easy to envision a group of youngsters enthusiastically creating scenes with their respective wheeled beasts.

ONFIM

Sweat dripped from his forehead and stung his eyes. His helmet was hot and stuffy and the sickly stench of decay and rot hung in the air around him. The landscape beyond him was a scorched, lifeless wasteland from which tendrils of smoke emitted from the still-smoldering rubble. The town that had stood here once—a small farming village on the outskirts of the kingdom—was unrecognizable from its former idyllic glory. The stone walls wove like black snakes through fields of ash, broken up by the shattered remains of homes whose burnt beams reached toward the sky like the teeth of an ancient beast.

It was not the first time he had come this way. Years ago, he had fought a great battle in these very fields, and he remembered it well. When armies of faceless enemies threw themselves upon him and his comrades like waves crashing on the rocks, he had broken them effortlessly. With each swing of his sword and stride of his horse, he worked to drive the forces of evil and tyranny away from the lands that he loved.

But this battle was different. There were no armies marching at his side. No pounding of war drums and no soldiers' songs. The ends of those stories lay littered across the countryside as crumpled masses of fused metal and charred bone. Today he was the only one, and when he set out from the kingdom's gate, he knew that was the way it must be. Finally, after days of following the trail of destruction on the back of his trusty steed, he laid eyes on that which had caused the decimation of the land he loved so much.

On the ridge he eased his stallion to a stop and gazed into the valley below. Along the riverbank plodded a creature unlike anything he had ever seen. It walked on four legs that stood like the trunks of the strongest trees, with massive feet that could rotate in any direction.

Its body was long and thin and continued into a tail that writhed and coiled like a snake. At the top of its towering neck was a head capped with two pointy, almost feline ears, and a mouth filled with razor-sharp teeth. It was from this mouth that the destruction had been wrought, for The Wild Beast could breathe fire.

He let out a quiet sigh. This was it. The grand finale. He stroked the silky black mane of his companion and, slowly, he lifted his helmet from his head and let it fall into the mud below. He closed his eyes and took a deep breath as the cool breeze ruffled his hair. His eyes opened. He drew his sword and, blade held high, thundered into the valley below.

Around 1260, in the medieval city of Novgorod, lived a boy named Onfim. It is believed that he was around six or seven years old. The anaerobic mud outside the city has, through archaeological excavation, yielded twelve of Onfim's *beresti* (singular: *beresta*), works that exude personality. Made of a single, thinly cut sheet of birch bark, beresta acts in almost the same way as wood-pulp paper. The difference is that it does not require manufacturing and is therefore far less expensive as it literally grows on trees.

The people of Novgorod produced countless documents over the course of the city's one-thousand-plus years of existence. Many of Onfim's papers are homework, some showing that he was in the process of learning to read and write in the old Slavonic dialect of Novgorodian. But, like anyone at the age of six who has been told to sit and write for long periods of time, Onfim grew bored.

One document bears the first eleven letters of the alphabet in the Slavic dialect of Old Novgorodian. After this point, the schoolboy grew tired of this task and resorted to drawing himself on horseback spearing a downed enemy. It's a majestic drawing that takes up more of the page than the original assignment, in true school-age-boy

ANAEROBIC ENVIRONMENTS

The mud in which these beresti were found is what is known as an anaerobic environment. Namely due to its lack of oxygen, these conditions make it highly difficult for bacteria to grow. As a result, the bark sheets have hardly decayed and look almost as they did the day they were buried. Anaerobic (or anoxic, if in water) environments are a treasure trove for archaeologists. Their conditions make the perfect place to inhibit decomposition, allowing for the preservation of everything from paper to shipwrecks to bog bodies.

fashion. He even went so far as to ensure we knew who the hero was, proudly labeling the mounted rider "Onfim," a fantasy projection of guts and glory that transcends time. These are not his only battle scenes, either, as two more of his birch-bark sheets depict three mounted riders charging into battle and a rider being chased by two men riding a shockingly long six-legged horse. Adorably, the mismatched numbers of fingers on his characters' hands have led some to believe that, while he was working on his writing, he still struggled with arithmetic.

An apparent socialite, Onfim even included his friends and family in his masterpieces. One piece, depicting a giant fire-breathing creature bearing the label "I am a wild beast" (the inspiration for my story above), is signed off with "Greetings from Onfim to Danilo." Whether the original intent had been to create a gift, it seems like Onfim decided that the person who would benefit the most from his "wild beast" was his friend Danilo! His work also includes depictions of family, most adorably a tiny Onfim standing next to his identical, yet larger, father. A timeless reminder of the inspiration for many young heroes.

HOPSCOTCH

A large portion of my time writing this book was spent at my local library, which served as a workspace free of distractions. Every day on my walk home I would pass a distinctive landmark left on the sidewalk by some of the kids in the neighborhood. A series of ten numbered squares that are part of a game that many of us know as hopscotch. While most days I strode past this grid without a second thought, there were several occasions when I impulsively flamingo-hopped from one end to the other to break up the monotony of the walk home. Little did I know that this game has its roots in antiquity.

As the story goes, the game of hopscotch can trace its roots to the Roman Empire some two thousand years ago. Part of the core of Rome's military might was their training practices, which ensured their armies were coordinated, fit, and equipped. Part of this rigorous training regime was a nearly 100-foot (30 m) track that involved navigating one's footsteps between a long line of squares, all while encumbered with the standard pack and equipment that each soldier had to carry. This exercise enhanced the soldiers' ability to be nimble on their feet and is akin to exercises done by modern athletes to improve coordination, such as jumping rope or doing a tire run. With such a massive percentage of its population in the army, it wasn't long before this exercise escaped from the Roman training camps and onto the bustling streets, where it was picked up by children.

Quickly the game was simplified, becoming a shorter track that was more conducive to a game rather than a workout. A scoring

THE ENCYCLOPEDIA OF THE WEIRD AND WONDERFUL

HOPSCOTCH AROUND THE WORLD

Like many other forms of entertainment, such as mancala (see page 96), it will come as no surprise to you that there are numerous variations of hopscotch found in many parts of the world from India to Brazil. I am not one to hypothesize the dispersal of this game, or claim whether or not some parts of the world developed it independently, but instead I can tell you just some of the many versions of it. In Iran there is *laylay*, in Germany it is known as *Himmel und Holle*, Ghana has *tumatu*, and in Scotland it is called peevers. Each game has slight variations that make it unique from the rest, but all are part of the hopscotch family that has kept children entertained for centuries.

system was added by numbering the squares on the ground, and before long the commandeered military drill had blossomed into a children's street game. By the 1600s, written records began to crop up referring to the game of "scotch-hop," which was, for all intents and purposes, the exact same thing as the modern-day hopscotch. The game continues to be popular amongst children on sidewalks around the world. On your next walk, should you pass one of these distinctive courses, think of how many "hops" this game has inspired within the last two thousand years. And if you are feeling particularly enthusiastic, spare ten hops to add to this ancient story.

THE QUEEN OF THE TOY STORE

Dolls are truly the uncontested champion of children's toys. In one form or another, dolls have been a staple of entertainment since time immemorial. They have been made of corn husks, clay, and, of course, porcelain—with their nightmare-inducing stares. But through all of their diversity there is one doll that reigns supreme above the rest in its popularity, influence, and mass production. It is none other than the immensely popular Barbie.

The brainchild of Ruth Handler, Barbies are the iconic line of plastic dolls manufactured by the toy company Mattel. Handler, along with her husband, found inspiration when they saw their daughter playing with another highly popular doll variant: paper dolls. The two determined that, while there were many options for children's dolls, they mostly centered around baby dolls and did little to facilitate a child's fantasy for what their future could be like. As a result, they worked to develop Barbie, or, her full name: Barbara Millicent Roberts. By the summer of 1959 the doll had begun its journey to becoming the icon it is today.

Barbie's release was met with a flurry of controversy. Some parents who saw the doll deemed her as too sexually provocative, with the emphasis on a slender feminine figure that was absent in all other children's toys at the time. Subsequently, many parents pushed back against the product and believed it to be inappropriate for their children. However, the ball was already rolling and, backed by Mattel, Handler was able to overcome this controversy by flooding the market and the airwaves with their new smash hit.

As luck (and clever business planning) would have it, Barbie was one of the first dolls to enter mass production, propelled onto store shelves en masse. Along with this, Mattel found a workaround to the adult apprehensions around this perceived adult doll: market it directly to children. With primetime advertising alongside companies like Disney, Mattel was able to market Barbie to their target audience unchallenged, in one of the first examples of mass advertising being directed solely at children. And, as you won't be surprised to hear, it worked. Within her first year, Barbie sold a staggering three hundred thousand dolls.

Barbie remains a staple of toy rooms and collectors' shelves alike. She has seen many iterations and additions to her cast, including her best friend, little sister, and of course her plastic, hunky boyfriend: Ken. To this day her flair for drama continues to burn, being the topic of countless studies and opinions surrounding the dolls' effect on the psychology of femininity. While many claim that Barbie dolls have helped empower them to think beyond gendered stereotypes of the late twentieth century, others insist that her form promotes unrealistic body expectations for women. A Finnish study even found that, if Barbara Millicent Roberts were a real woman, she would be so emaciated that she would be unable to menstruate.

While the effects she has had on people will likely be debated ceaselessly, it is undeniable that no other doll has had quite as profound an impact as Barbie.

CHAPTER 2

EAT, DRINK, AND BE MERRY

✦ ✦ ✦

One of the most important shared traditions within every culture around the world is the act of sharing a meal. While simple, sitting down to have food with friends, family, or members of the community has been a staple part of the human bonding experience for our entire existence on this planet. From our earliest ancestors sharing a day's hunt over a fire beneath the stars to last weekend's potluck dinner party with your friends, this tradition has gone through many iterations but still remains the same at its core.

THE HALLSTATT STEW

On the awe-inspiring slopes of Austria's Salzkammergut region lie the remains of nearly seven thousand years of human history. This region is known as the Hallstatt Valley and has such a prolific and well-preserved human presence that the region lent its name to define a time period: the Hallstatt Period. One of the largest motivators for ancient people to come to the area was the presence of a massive salt mine complex that existed in the mountains around 3,500 years ago.

This mine is beyond impressive, with tunnels running 560 feet (170 m) long, 65 feet (20 m) high and 82 feet (25 m) wide in places. The skill and technological understanding required to complete a task like this with bronze tools is mind-blowing. But this network of ancient, salty tunnels has had a unique implication for modern archaeologists: the fact that the air in these ancient tunnels has preserved natural material to a startling degree.

Within the mine systems, archaeologists have found not only human coprolites but also ancient food that has remained underground for nearly four thousand years. Amongst this haul have been found wooden boxes with the remains of cheese inside, hazelnut shells, wooden spoons, and clay cookery. With so many clues left underground, it was possible for archaeologists to recreate the meal that the miners ate to sustain their hard work all those years ago.

Coprolites have shown that miners were eating barley and broad beans, as well as broken pieces of bone originating from hooves or other undesirable meat cuts. This combination of foods would have provided miners with the carbs, protein, and fats they needed to sustain their work. With the context of bowls, cooking pots, and spoons also found at the site, it is likely that this food was prepared as some form of stew. Through shifting cultures, climates, and technologies, this stew recipe has persisted. In Austria's Salzkammergut region, one can still get a hearty bowl of this stew, called Ritschert, which is made with beans, grain, and bones and is nearly the same as the food prepared in the region thousands of years before.

COPROLITES

The study of coprolites is much more exciting than it sounds. While it may seem rather unpleasant, the study of ancient feces can tell us a lot about the world that ancient people lived in. For example, coprolites can be studied to understand diets by analyzing the physical remains left behind. It can also be an indicator of health, potentially holding the remains of parasites or other signs of illness. They may not be flashy, but coprolites are a treasure trove of information!

BONE STEW

One of my personal favorite meals is beef stew. Growing up in the biting New England winters, it was not uncommon for me to find myself devouring a bowl of the hearty homemade goodness after a day of hiking, sledding, or spelunking. I would be willing to bet that you too have a fond memory of a homemade stew that graced your family's dinner table a handful of times out of the year that left you feeling full, warm, and exhausted. The tradition of soups and stews is not unique to us. It goes back tens of thousands of years.

Just one of these many examples comes from a two-thousand-year-old vessel discovered near the Shaanxi Province's capital of Xi'an, in northwestern China. Buried along the deceased occupant of a tomb from around 350 BCE were two bronze pots of different sizes. The smaller of the two pots contained an ancient liquid that is believed to have been the remains of alcohol, potentially wine. The larger of the two pots, on the other hand, contained a remarkably well-preserved meal: the still-liquid remains of a soup that had been placed in it more than two thousand years ago. Among the floating pieces of bronze that had flaked off over the years were the remains of several bones. Archaeologists believe that the bones once belonged to either a chicken, rabbit, or other small game animal. After millennia in the ground, the bones have become so saturated with the oxidized metal that they share the green color of the bronze rust, creating what appears more as a greenish bone slurry than a stew.

While more research is needed to understand the ceremony further, it is theorized that the burial of food and alcohol alongside the deceased was a common practice at this time. It is merely by a stroke of lucky preservation that this ancient meal was able to survive almost intact.

FOOD FROZEN IN TIME

The man stepped through the doorway and announced his arrival with an exhausted, "It's me." He stomped his sandals off and removed his apron. From the other room emerged his wife, carrying their daughter in her arms. She strode over to him and planted a kiss on his cheek as he hung his apron on the peg by the door.

"Well? How was the day?" she asked, adjusting the squirming baby who was swaddled in a piece of linen.

"Exactly the same as the last one. And the one before that," he said frustratedly as he knelt to remove his well-worn leather sandals. "That damn kid is useless! I give him the simple task to fire the oven before I get there. Just a tiny thing. Quite literally one of his only jobs. And he *still* shows up late!" He ended with a huff and tossed off one of his shoes. It flopped against the base of the plaster wall before slumping onto the wide flagstones that made up the floor of the little home.

"Oh, I am sorry, honey. That is awfully frustrating," she responded in a compassionate tone.

"And it gets better!" he continued, beginning his assault on his second sandal. "So, the kid is late, does not start the fire, I have to do it *all* myself, and by the time I even get bread in the oven there are five or six regulars inside waiting on me!" Still kneeling, he had abandoned his shoe and was talking equally with his mouth and his hands. "I have standards in my business, and I will *never*–" he swooshed his arms through the air for emphasis– "have my regulars waiting on me." He resumed work on his shoe with a frustrated sigh. It, like the rest of him, was caked in flour, and the lengthy removal process sent up delicate puffs of white dust into the evening air.

Kneeling on the floor next to him, his wife wrapped her free arm around his shoulders. "That is very frustrating, and I am sorry to hear that it spoiled your day. Have you considered looking for a new assistant?"

"Absolutely! That kid is useless! There are plenty of bakers in this city and I will not lose my valuable customers to my competition because of a lazy teenager. I take this job very seriously and have three mouths to feed. No one is getting in the way of that."

"And thank you for all you do, my love." She kissed him on the top of his head and stood up. He closed his eyes, let out a grounding sigh, gently placed his last sandal next to the other, and rose to embrace her.

When they parted, his face was alight. "And!" he said excitedly, "look what I got!"

He rummaged in his sheepskin bag and pulled out a clay pot, which he presented to her on the small wooden table. Opening the lid with a flourish, he said, "Pork and lentils! From Marius's place across the way. We were talking about our days after work, and he gave us this! Thought it would make for a nice dinner."

"Aha!" She was delighted. "That is too kind! I will have to remember to thank him next time I see him."

"And . . . " he continued, slowly reaching into the bag again, "Sweet cakes!" He pulled two rolls from the bag, golden brown and slathered with honey.

The baby giggled excitedly and reached toward them. Despite not having the teeth to chew, Mom and Dad had been steadily supplying the little one with fingers of honey from these treats (this was back in the days when parents didn't know you shouldn't feed a baby honey).

"Incredible!" the wife responded. "Well, you have had a long day. Why don't you go wash your face and change out of those work clothes and we can dine?"

"A fantastic idea." The husband gave her a kiss on the forehead before striding away to freshen up.

———————————

It would be functionally impossible to make it through this book without mentioning Pompeii at least once. The ancient Roman city has such an immensely well-preserved archaeological record that it has transcended the status of archaeological site and is now a world-famous location, one that provides a unique view back in time that can be found in few other parts of the world. Frankly, I think there is no better place to do this than while discussing the story of human cuisine.

While Pompeii can tell a story about nearly all aspects of human life from its rubble, the evidence of food has been particularly extensive. Since food is typically a product that decays quickly, the unique burial of Pompeii has allowed for traditionally delicate foodstuffs to survive almost two thousand years. Among the ruined streets of the city are more than eighty food vendors: booths that once prepared and sold food to passersby. Think of it like an ancient food truck. Some of the booths discovered are brightly painted with images of chickens, ducks, amphorae, and olive branches. Some theorize that these brightly colored paintings could have acted like a menu, informing people as to what types of food the vendor had for sale. Some of these were slightly less literal, like a stall that displayed a fresco of a nymph riding a seahorse on its counter and was found with the remains of broken earthenware with fish bones and snail shells. This suggests that these "menus" could also be a bit of an artistic or thematic interpretation of the types of food for sale rather than a specific and itemized menu that we have today.

It is easy to view these ancient restaurants as mystical places, but they were quite like today's street food or fast food. The vendors' stalls had depressions in the front counter that likely acted to display food that was for sale, reminiscent of today's DIY burrito, bowl, or sandwich shop. The foods that have been found include pork, duck, goat, chicken, loaves of bread, olives, wine, lentils, and even eggs whose fragile shells remained intact and preserved through the hellfire of volcanic destruction. The preservation of material like this is incredible. Loaves of bread, now black carbonized discs, still bear stamps from the baker who prepared it two thousand years ago.

By looking at the context in which this food was found, we can see that these streets were once home to a bustling community of hungry people. Not stuffy aristocrats as we so often view the Romans, but people like you and me who wove through crowded city streets soaked in the hunger-inducing smells of roast duck, fresh baked bread, and hearty stew.

CHAMPAGNE OF THE SEA

Humankind holds champagne in high regard. For most people, it is a treat used to celebrate a wedding, graduation, new year, or other milestone. The delicate flavor and delightful bubbles make it unlike many other alcoholic drinks, solidifying it as a mainstay among the ranks of humanity's iconic beverages. There are, however, 168 bottles of champagne that have a story like no other.

In 2010, a group of divers happened across the shattered hull of a shipwreck at the bottom of the Baltic Sea. Littered among the debris was some of the ship's still-preserved cargo: nearly 200 bottles of French champagne that had lain on the seafloor for 170 years. Incredibly, the bottles were still sealed and their contents unadulterated by the salt water around them. Meaning that they were, in theory, still drinkable.

But before researchers broke out the champagne flutes, there was more research to be done. While the labels on the bottles as well as the crates they were held in had long since deteriorated on the seafloor, the bottles still had labels stamped on the bottom of their corks that had survived unscathed. (Also, as an aside, the corks survived. How insane is that?) Some of the bottles were produced by brands that still operate today, including Veuve Clicquot Ponsardin, which is the second highest-selling champagne in the world.

Since the bottles were sealed and the contents were alcoholic, they were theoretically still safe to drink. Researchers did find that there were higher levels of copper and iron in the wine, which is likely due to the manufacturing process as well as the copper sulfate that was used as a fungicide at the time, but in small quantities, it was potable.

And drink it they did! These antique bottles of seafloor-aged wine have sold for upward of *one hundred thousand dollars* and became a highly sought-after flavor amongst the elite champagne-ists of the world. The flavor was described as "grilled, spicey, smokey, and leathery" according to a paper published on it, which sounds more like the description of mezcal or beef jerky than of champagne. In response to this discovery, there has even been some strides taken to see if the underwater aging process can be replicated to allow these unique flavors and aromas to be enjoyed by people like you and me.

HOW NOT TO MAKE WINE

Since its discovery, alcohol has been a staple in just about every major culture and tradition around the world. Because of this, humanity has formed quite a strong relationship with this delightfully poisonous beverage over the past thousands of years. As a result, we really don't like it when our special drink is taken away from us.

One of the largest recent examples of this is, of course, Prohibition. This insane chapter in American history saw the passing of the Eighteenth Amendment, which prohibited the sale, manufacture, and distribution of alcohol from 1920 until 1933, when the Twenty-First Amendment overruled it. In 1915, before Prohibition, the average American had thirteen drinks a week, totaling up to nearly 2½ gallons of pure alcohol over the course of a year. Needless to say, the outright banning of alcoholic drinks made a lot of people *very* unhappy. But humans are a problem-solving species, so when you back us into a corner, we will almost always find a way to weasel our way out of it. From speakeasies to moonshiners, the stories of Prohibition-avoiders are plentiful. But my personal favorite comes in a tidy, brick-shaped package.

As Prohibition kicked into full swing, stores began to carry a brick-like package of condensed grapes. These packages bore a specific (if tongue-in-cheek) warning on the back that read along the lines of:

"Whatever you do, don't dissolve this brick in water, cover it and leave it in a closet for 20 days because then it would turn into wine . . . ;)"

You'll never guess what happened next.

People started turning it into wine! And not just a few people, I mean a *ton* of people started to explore the wonderful world of home-brewed booze. Some of these highly conspicuous packages even advertised different flavors, such as brandy. Between 1917 and 1925, Americans went from consuming around 70 million gallons (265 million L) of wine to consuming *150* million gallons (567 million L) of wine. A number that is also likely skewed due to some under-reporting. This caused a ridiculous demand for grapes that were mostly grown in the California agricultural belt. Prices for the little fruits skyrocketed, with a ton of grapes that had been worth around $10 before Prohibition now being valued at around $350. This became so profitable that entire wineries built their empires around this loophole in the Eighteenth Amendment.

One of our best traits as a species is our ability to find ways around the rules. Our creativity can manifest wonderful things—from architecture to technological marvels—but there is nothing quite as hilarious as a nationwide operation dedicated to exploiting a legal loophole so that a New York City mom can have a glass of wine.

ALICANTE BELIEVE IT!

As California was hit with its first wine boom, countless new vineyards opened to capitalize on a new demand. But this "brick wine" was not like the countless flavors and aromas we have in our grocery stores today. Since it involved shipping grapes in a solid form, vineyards had to choose their grapes accordingly, which is why many went with the Alicante grape. It was a tough, resilient, and dense red grape that survived packaging and transport well. However, when Prohibition ended, vineyards were left with a monoculture (totaling over forty thousand acres!) of one type of grape that just sort of sucked at making normal wine. As a result, California wineries had a massive bust after Prohibition, as they planted crops that would produce more profitable and tasty finished products.

WORK WITH WHAT YOU GOT

There is no such thing as strange food, merely food you have never heard of or don't eat in your culture. There are plenty of foods that have ingredients, preparations, and cultural significance that are unique to certain parts of the world. While many of these may seem strange in comparison to the foods we eat in the United States, these unusual dishes stand as a testament to the resilience of humanity. No matter what point of the compass we ended up in, people found a way to utilize their surroundings to sustain themselves, and in doing so paved the way for those who came after them. Given that we live in an ever-globalized world, I think it's important to highlight some of these dishes that showcase the adaptability of our species.

KIVIAK

Hailing from the Inuit people of Greenland, this unique food is different in both preparation and ingredients from most other dishes on the planet. This winter dish consists of one seal and the bodies of around five hundred little auks—a small, seagull-like bird that is native to the North Atlantic. The preparation of kiviak is . . . simple.

The five hundred seabirds are put inside the body of the seal in their entirety—we are talking about beaks, feathers, feet, and all the other delightful odds and ends that make a bird. Once they have been comfortably stuffed inside the seal, the carcass is sewn shut and slathered with seal fat to prevent flies from getting into it. The entire amalgam is then buried for a few months to allow it to ferment.

Once fermentation is complete, the birds from the inside of the seal carcass are eaten. Being a complicated food to prepare, these stinky seabirds are consumed as a part of celebrations and are more of a delicacy than a staple. During this process everything but the feathers and bones can be, and are, eaten. The "juice" left over is also consumed and used as a sauce or flavoring. From my research it has been described as having a flavor like "very mature cheese." Delicious!

While this may seem unsavory to a Western audience, it is important to note the context to understand why a dish like this was developed. Greenland is rather barren, making food scarce. Being able to stock up on seabirds when they are plentiful and before they migrate, as well as have a place to store them for months without them going bad, is a highly effective adaptation to surviving potential winter food shortages. This unique dish is still prepared for brave tourists and traditional consumers alike.

THIS LITTLE PIGGY

When I was growing up, I had the opportunity to tag along with my dad to Ecuador, where he was on a historic preservation assignment. While there are many aspects of the country that stood out, there was one experience that I remember very well: the sight of a food vendor serving skewered, spit-roasted guinea pigs. While this dish makes abundant sense to me as an adult, as a child I was shocked. The only time I had seen guinea pigs before that was in pet stores and my friends' homes, where their contented "gweep" noise acted as a constant reminder to their presence.

Called *cuy*, which just translates to "guinea pig," it is a popular dish from Peru to Bolivia to Ecuador. The dish has myriad ways in which it can be served; typically cooked whole, the preparation of these critters can be anything from spit-roasting, deep-frying, or even compression between two hot stones. The seasoned and crisped cuy is often served alongside corn and potatoes and makes up an important part of the South American diet.

The history of this dish dates back as far as human habitation itself, with evidence of cuy being consumed upward of five thousand years ago. Indigenous Andean peoples enjoyed this delicacy just as much as modern inhabitants do today. The cultural impact of cuy is widespread across the region, with festivals held that celebrate the fluffy beasts. Places like Churin, in Peru, have an annual celebration that involves dressing up live animals in colorful and extravagant costumes, and there is even a mural in the Cusco Cathedral depicting Jesus dining on cuy at the Last Supper!

So why cuy? If you are from a culture that does not partake in this dish it may seem like an alien concept. Once again, we have to drop our predisposition around what is "strange" and what isn't. Firstly, these animals are native to the Andes, meaning that they are essentially the equivalent of rabbits. Secondly, they are *very* easy to keep in captivity and will live a happy life with a full belly from all the food scraps that no one else wants. And finally, they breed like . . . well . . . guinea pigs, and can produce up to six offspring per litter.

Cuy is not only an economic and nutritious food source, but it is also an important part of local cuisine and culture. If I ever find myself in Ecuador again, I will be paying a street food vendor a visit with my newfound appreciation for these adorable and delicious little critters.

THERE'S A BAT IN MY SOUP

Bats are great. Little flying guys whose skeletons look like funny tiny dudes with big, long fingers. They eat pest insects, naturally produce an incredible fertilizer, and spend the evenings clicking to their heart's content. You'd have to be a fool to not love a good old-fashioned bat. But the inhabitants of the island of Palau take enjoying a good old-fashioned bat to levels that most never dreamed possible.

Residents of the culturally rich Republic of Palau have a unique dish known as fruit bat soup. You would be correct in assuming that it is exactly what it sounds like. This delicacy's namesake ingredient is one of the fruit bats that reside on the forests of this remote island. The dish is prepared with spices such as ginger, leafy greens, and a base of coconut milk and water. While the dish can be prepared in a multitude of ways depending on the chef, the *pièce de résistance* is the entire fruit bat complete with skin, wings, fur, and head in the soup.

For those of us who do not eat this dish regularly, this can obviously be rather shocking. In a review I read of it online while researching this book, the waitress serving the dish, who was presumably used to the traumatized gasp of traveling Western food writers coming face to face with a boiled bat, took it upon herself to take the bat out of the soup and prepare it at the table after getting the initial shock factor. Comedically, her preparation involved sticking long peppers into the bat's eye sockets and mouth to make it look like some sort of leathery hellspawn. Delicious! Obviously, this dish is not for the faint of heart, with even its flavor being described as a bit like a redder meat tuna. But it is important to understand why this dish exists at all.

Palau is a small island chain, around 180 square miles (5 m^2) in total. It suffers from many of the setbacks that tropical islands pose to the groups that inhabit them. There is minimal freshwater, residents are isolated far from all other major landmasses, fertile soil is scarce, and there is far from a limitless supply of terrestrial food. As a result, the Palauan people had to adapt to this hostile environment to ensure their continued success. Bat soup is just one of these adaptations: a calorie-dense, high-protein food that can be made with an animal that was in virtually limitless supply in the island's jungles. While it may seem strange today, we must remember that this dish is, in actuality, an ingenious adaptation that allowed for continued success in a harsh environment.

THE END OF THE SILK ROAD

There are countless places around the world that have insects as part of their diet. Being prolific, nutritious, and versatile enough to be prepared in any texture and flavor you want, the idea of using bugs as food is a phenomenal one. Just one of the many examples of bug dishes around the world is the South Korean dish known as *beondegi.* The name translates to "pupae" in Korean, which makes sense considering that that is exactly what this dish consists of: silkworm pupae!

The larvae are prepared by either steaming them or boiling them in a large pan. Beondegi is a popular street food that can often be purchased by the paper cup out of the large pans of streetside vendors. The dish makes the final branch of its journey from the cup to your mouth by way of skewering the pupae with a toothpick! These little snacks are apparently rather chewy and have an earthy flavor to them. If that doesn't float your boat, there is also *beondegi-tang*, a soup made with garlic, soy sauce, onions, and plenty of other aromatic ingredients, which features the pupae as its protein. While many cultures have traditions of eating insects that date back to near eternity, the story of these larvae is actually rather unique.

While it is likely that this food has been eaten since as long as people knew about silkworms and had an appetite, this dish's modern history traces back to the Korean War. When the reliability of good sources of protein declined as a result of the conflict, the Korean population were forced to adapt in whatever way they could. People left with few options began to eat the larvae, as it is a highly nutritious food source that is packed with protein. After the war ended, the tradition continued, with the dish being refined and perpetuated. It was from the resilience of the human spirit that this modern street food was born.

UNHOLY BALONEY

Humanity is defined by our hubris. Our oldest stories tell tales of insolent and arrogant people being wiped from the Earth by the wrath of an angry deity. Stories like the Tower of Babel, Icarus, and

Atlantis all warn us that contempt against the ways of nature will be punished. While we have a pretty good track record of creating crimes against the planet itself–from nuclear weapons to mandatory minimum sentencing–there is one single creation that stands as nothing more than a testament to our desire to spit in the face of God. That, of course, is baloney.

Baloney is a crime. It is the embodiment of humanity's insolence against natural processes. Our single most repulsive creation. Baloney, the Americanized version at least, can be made with pork, beef, or even chicken. And at times, like in the case of, hypothetically, Oscar Mayer's product, all three at once. The Frankenmeat gets its start as the least-profitable scraps left over on the butchered remains of some animal that spent its life in a feedlot. Deliciously, this nearly useless meat is referred to as "raw skeletal muscle." It is also combined with edible organs such as hearts and livers. The whole thing is pulverized, pureed, and combined with the bowel-cancer-causing preservative sodium nitrate (seriously, look for this in all the meat you buy, it's everywhere), then garnished with some spices so it can pretend to be food and be squeezed into the unholy cylinder shape that we know and love. But how did this happen? What is the purpose? Why would a merciful God allow this to happen? All great questions. The answer begins, as many great things do, in Italy.

This dish originated from mortadella, an Italian minced pork sausage from the Bologna region. Allegedly, the original dish was prepared by using a mortar and pestle (*mortaio* in Italian) and is supposedly where the name comes from.

When Italian immigrants came to America, the dish was passed on to German immigrants in the Midwest who added their own spin to it. Today this food has changed so much from its original style that it is practically unrecognizable. Just remember as you go through life to be humble, because once we start to get cocky, we do things like this.

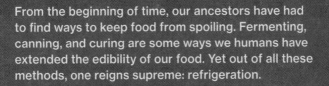

NO SPOIL-ERS

From the beginning of time, our ancestors have had to find ways to keep food from spoiling. Fermenting, canning, and curing are some ways we humans have extended the edibility of our food. Yet out of all these methods, one reigns supreme: refrigeration.

Humanity's journey to the appliance that keeps our leftovers cold until they get "accidentally" taken by our siblings has been nothing short of ingenious. The ancient Persians invented a towering, dome-shaped ice-house structure called a *yakhchal*, which was a sort of ancient refrigerator that could keep ice frozen in the winter and allow the Persians to store food in the warmer months, not to mention enjoy a cold drink or two. Fast forward a couple of centuries and technological advances later to the 1930s, and people could install electric cooling devices in their homes! The flexibility in what we eat and when is a direct result of adapting to our surroundings and utilizing our creativity, an enduring idea that is still conveniently used to sell refrigerators today.

CHAPTER 3
OUR BEST FRIENDS

✦ ✦ ✦

There are two kinds of people in this world: those who say they love animals, and liars. Something about the fluffy, scaly, and feathered beasts we share this planet with has always spoken to us. Perhaps it's because we see a bit of ourselves in them, or simply that we like having company. Our companions have been many: a mutt that paced alongside the builders of the Cahokia Mounds, feline royalty in an ancient Egyptian temple, and the countless other animals that have always been humankind's best friends.

RATS OF THE SKY: THE RISE
AND FALL OF THE PIGEON

You would be hard pressed to find an animal with a worse reputation than the pigeon. They are seen as pests, disease carriers, and the serial defecators of city sidewalks across the world. Perhaps the only animal with a more negative global reputation is the rat, a creature that many view in such a similar light to the pigeon that the gray birds have been given the nickname "rats with wings." Mankind has not looked kindly upon these sweet and social birds, but after seeing countless pigeons in every city across the planet, one must pause to ask, "Why?" How did this North African bird end up being a hallmark of places like Boston, London, and Sydney? The answer, my friend, is us.

As you may be surprised to know, humanity domesticated pigeons! Written records of this relationship date back as far as writing itself, with evidence of pigeon domestication on five-thousand-year-old cuneiform tablets. Many archaeologists, myself included, believe that this relationship is actually much older, potentially dating back upward of ten thousand years to around when many parts of the Middle East began the domestication of other more well-known domestic animals such as goats, cattle, and cats. Originally these birds were bred for food, but their role soon expanded to become messengers, companions, and even fancy showbirds!

When the colonization of North America began, pigeons (after a multiple-thousand-year relationship with humans) booked a ticket across the pond and set their little orange feet on *terra firma* in the early 1600s alongside pigs, cattle, and geese. And as the young country of America absorbed the continent, the pigeon tagged along, taking roost in treetops and rafters alongside their human companions.

But by the beginning of the 1900s that relationship had changed. Industry dominated the country and the need for pigeons had waned. Plus, most major cities now housed the largest populations in the form of feral birds who descended from escapees or were abandoned. Around this time the attitude toward birds changed, and after being blamed for the death of two individuals in New York City in the early 1960s, humanity officially turned their back on the little birds.

It is thus that after ten thousand years of human domestication, affection, and specialization, we have all but abandoned these little birds over the course of three generations. They helped us win wars by flying messages over shell-strewn fields, fed our people when food ran low, and earned awards and praise for their fancy plumage and curious personalities. Yet today they are seen as no more than pests. So I ask you, my dear reader, that next time you commute to work and happen across one of these plucky little fliers, greet it not with disdain or animosity, but with the appreciation of two species that would be nothing without each other.

PULLING HIS WEIGHT

Humankind has a history of interacting with the other creatures of this Earth that dates back nigh on eternally. The topic of the domestication of various species is one that is as fascinating as it is nuanced. While I may not be qualified to discuss the true origins of dog domestication or the genetic evidence that allows us to learn about the wild ancestor of cats, I am qualified to take you back to some of the oldest concrete evidence we have of a dog who lived and worked alongside humans. He was a strong breed, likely resembling a modern husky or a Tamaskan, and lived around seven thousand years ago along the banks of what is today called Lake Baikal, in Russia.

Evidence of wear on the dog's spine indicates that his life had been spent hauling materials and tools alongside his owners, as much a part of the village team as everyone else. For his help as a member of the community, he was fed like a member of the community. Isotopic analysis of his bones show that he had eaten a diverse selection of food such as fish, seal, deer, and even plant material. All the food that would have been gathered—and shared—by the human members of the community.

This ancient work dog highlights a unique time in domestication history. An ancestor who likely acted as a loyal companion just as many of our canine compatriots, this particular pooch lived at a time when man's best friend was still strikingly similar to their wild counterparts, the menacing and majestic wolf. While he may have laid his

LAKE BAIKAL

I must pause for a second to tell you about this lake. I know this isn't really archaeology or history, but I am as much of a fanatic for Earth science and geology as the aforementioned, so bear with me because this lake is insane.

Lake Baikal is the largest freshwater lake in the world by volume (5,500 cubic miles, or 23,000 km³ of water) and holds not only more water than all of the Great Lakes combined, but also 20 percent of the fresh surface water on the entire planet! It is the oldest freshwater lake on Earth at twenty-five million years old, and is the deepest freshwater lake, reaching depths of 5,300 feet (1,600 m). It also has geothermal springs, earthquakes, and is home to its own species of fish called the golomyanka, which gives birth to live young and looks like what a marine biologist sees while under the influence of an industrial-grade hallucinogen.

While all the information we have about this Neolithic pooch comes from his burial, we know a huge amount about the life that he lived. The burial itself was a tender affair. Laid to rest on his side, the dog was accompanied by an antler spoon as a grave good, an artifact displaying a high level of craftsmanship and skill. This suggests that the human owners had cared less about the value of the item and more about ensuring that their companion had a good send-off to the great beyond.

head down for the last time many thousand years ago, this dog was, in effect, the ancient grandfather to the German shepherds, poodles, and pugs that delight people across the globe today.

THE DOGS OF TURTLE ISLAND

Dogs feature a lot in this chapter, but they are truly the uncontested crown jewels of humans' desire to bend the forces of nature to their will. Dogs have been bred for everything from hunting to hauling to stunting. It is truly incredible the amount of diversity we have managed to coax out of this single species, not just in our standard European breeds, but all over the world.

North America was home to many breeds of dogs before the Columbian Exchange. Like their modern counterparts, they had been bred for myriad tasks and were a vital part of the Indigenous and Paleo-Indigenous communities of what is now known as North America. Here is where one would assume to see a laundry list of the diverse breeds that made up this continental pooch pack, but one would be disappointed to find that this is not so. As is the case with nearly everything in North America, European contact was nothing short of a disaster. These various dog breeds were decimated by a combination of diseases such as rabies and distemper, hungry colonizers, and simply the fact that they were seen as vermin by those who bore muskets and pikes. With little effort made to document these countless breeds, many of them have been lost to history.

Most of our evidence of these dogs comes only from skeletal remains that litter the continent, from the Hare Indian dog to the little Salish Wool dog. Some, like the Tahltan bear dog, existed all the way up to the 1970s before its genetic pool fizzled out, putting an end to a species that had been specifically bred to traverse snowy crust

in packs to hunt bears. But there are a handful that remain. Breeds like the Carolina dog, Alaskan Malamute, and Xoloitzcuintli (more commonly referred to as the Mexican hairless dog) still exist today, the final survivors who have risen strong against every attempt to wipe them from the face of the Earth.

A TOMB FIT FOR A DOG

The sun scorched the desert below. The sweat that had been beading on Meryre's brow condensed, running down his face and falling in a large drop from the tip of his nose. It landed on the limestone block in front of him with a soft plop. He let out a deep sigh and craned his head upward, stretching his neck and rolling back his aching shoulders. He tilted his head to the side to see Harsiese, his friend, emerging from the throng of workers with an enormous grin on his face.

"Looks like you are having the time of your life over here!" he shouted, with his arms outstretched. Meryre wiped his brow with the back of his hand and tossed his chisel into the sand with a scoff.

"Look at this!" he exclaimed, gesturing with both hands to the slab that lay before him. Harsiese stopped by his side, braced his hands on his knees, and doubled over to inspect the work. They both peered down like two prospectors searching for a speck of gold.

Before the pair sat a slab of stone on which an image was beginning to appear. It showed a dog on a leash held in the hand of a man whose form had only begun to take shape that morning and was woefully unfinished.

"What is it?" Harsiese asked after a moment.

"A dog!"

SPOLIA

Spolia is the archaeological word for "upcycle," or, more bluntly, "building out of garbage." This practice involves repurposing old buildings, roads, and other built materials for use in new constructions. Examples of it can be found across the world, from medieval buildings made with Roman columns to the repurposed barn wood under a suburban mom's "live laugh love" wall art. While it may be a great use of premade material, it can be a nightmare for context with countless structures from countless time periods finding themselves smashed together like an archaeological Frankenstein's monster.

"A dog?"

"Yes! I am making a carving for the tomb of a dog!"

Harsiese looked at him slowly with an eyebrow raised, then threw his head back and roared with laughter.

"I have been doing this for fifteen years!" Myrere yelled over his friend's raucous glee. "Fifteen years and they have me carving a slab for a dog!"

"Oh ho!" sputtered Harsiese, smearing tears of laughter across his cheek with his index finger. "That's wonderful! I see you have been promoted!"

"Don't rub it in," he said. "They should just be happy they are paying me enough for this."

"And who exactly is 'they' in this case?" Harsiese inquired. "I wasn't aware there was a market for such a thing!"

"Look!" the disgruntled mason yelled. "Read the damn rock!"

He jabbed a calloused finger at the hieroglyphs he was partway through carving. Harsiese squatted down, dusted off the slab, and read over the glyphs, muttering to himself as he went. His eyes opened wide as he read out loud " . . . His Majesty ordered him to be buried ceremonially . . . *His Majesty*?" After repeating the phrase to himself in disbelief he collapsed to the ground howling with laughter. "Oh, my friend! What an honor it is to bury His Majesty's dog! You are practically royalty!" he sputtered through bouts of laughter.

"You are an ass," grumbled Meryre and he kicked a pile of sand at his delighted companion.

THE ENCYCLOPEDIA OF THE WEIRD AND WONDERFUL

Still weak from laughter, Harsiese brought himself to a sitting position. He stood up and patted his friend on the back, chuckling. "Well, I'll let you get back to it, Your Majesty!" He sank to a deep bow before standing upright, grinning from ear to ear.

"You are dismissed," humored Meryre with an eye roll and a wave of his hand.

His friend began to walk off, brushing sand from his clothes and shaking his head as if to coax out the last of his laughter. He about-faced, and, pacing backwards, yelled back to his friend: "Still coming for beers later?"

"After *this*? You wouldn't be able to stop me if you wanted to!"

His friend whistled and threw his hands high into the air in confirmation before blending back into the throng. Meryre chuckled and let out a deep sigh, scooped his chisel from the sand and continued his work.

Dogs have frequently been referred to as man's best friend—and with good reason. You would struggle to meet someone who didn't have a fond memory with one of these personable companions, whether it be a childhood pet, a brief encounter on your morning walk, or the loving beast who, even though you tried to train them out of it, is sleeping on your couch next to you right now. While the history of canine domestication dates back to time immemorial, currently the oldest-known example of a dog who was given a name by his masters dates back to around 2250–2200 BCE.

In 1938, a Harvard-Boston expedition discovered the remains of a mastaba (an Egyptian mud-brick burial structure) while on an archaeological dig near the pyramid of Cheops, at Giza, Egypt. During the analysis of the spolia that made up the mastaba, archaeologists discovered a limestone tablet that bore the visage of a slender, pointy-eared dog on what appears to be a leash.

While weathered, the ancient slab of stone still bore a legible inscription, which was translated and shared in the *Journal of the Museum of Fine Arts, Boston* from the same year.

The slab introduces the dog as Abuwtyuw, who is described as some sort of royal guard dog. Along with this, it explains that "His Majesty" himself was responsible for the pooch's burial, going so far as to have him buried with ointment, incense, and even a linen shroud inside a custom-made coffin. Beyond this, the site into which the dog was laid to rest was built by a team of skilled masons and craftsmen, as per royal order. As the slab ends, it claims that these elaborate rituals were conducted in order to ensure that Abuwtyuw would be honored and recognized in the afterlife by the god Anubis.

While Abuwtyuw was a guard dog, the pomp and circumstance surrounding his burial indicates that he was viewed as far more than that. He had, like many of our beloved pets, transcended the role of pet or protector and was seen as a friend and member of the family.

The funerary rituals that Abuwtyuw experienced after death were unusually elaborate for a pet. While it was not uncommon in ancient Egypt for animals to be mummified (examples include cats, crocodiles, ibis, and baboons), the inclusion of grave goods such as

A DIFFERENT BREED

Abuwtyuw's breed has been the subject of debate since the discovery of this repurposed slab of stone. While we may never know the exact breed, it has been theorized that this loyal pooch was a tesem. This ancient breed of dog has no living examples and is solely relegated to the annals of Egyptian history. Tesem was a breed of Egyptian hunting dogs that were also used for their guarding prowess. They possessed long, slender bodies, thin tails, and pointy ears, making them quite comparable to the modern greyhound. Today all the tesem dogs that we can still see come in the form of mummies whose souls have gone on to join their masters in the afterlife, leaving behind only their mortal remains as a reminder of the loyal companions that they once were.

ointment, incense, and a custom-carved tomb is a level of opulence that was typically reserved for members of the elite and royalty. These measures all ensured that Abuwtyuw's Ka, or soul, would be able to join that of his master in the great beyond.

Everyone who has lost a pet knows how gut-wrenching of an experience it is. Loss is never easy, but the loss of a being that did nothing but good in their life is particularly devastating for all those who knew them. While the tomb of Abuwtyuw has never been found, there is something comforting that his name and story are still known more than four thousand years after his death. Wherever you are, Abuwtyuw, remember that you are a good boy.

THE BERENICE PET CEMETERY

Ancient Egypt is home to countless animal burials, with the aforementioned guard dog being one that stands out. However, there is another pet burial location in Egypt that I believe deserves its own section: the Berenice "Pet Cemetery." Located on the ancient Red Sea port of Berenice, in Egypt, this site has been hesitantly called "the oldest pet cemetery in the world." (Though due to a multitude of older burials throughout different parts of the world, that title is hotly contested.)

This unusual location has yielded the remains of 585 animals that were interred between the first and second centuries CE. The dog and cat remains at the site are numerous, making up nearly all of those recovered. Of these, the dog remains range from medium-sized long-haired dogs to lankier hunting dogs and even a handful of functionally "useless" but "awww-inspiring" miniature dogs. The remains of several different macaques were also found at the site, suggesting an interesting addition to the typical roster of pets.

What makes this site a cemetery more than a mass grave is the care that was demonstrated with each burial. Many of the animals were found bearing collars made of metal or beadwork, and some still bore the shrouds that they were buried in as well as grave goods such as pottery. Further analysis of these animals has shown that some were afflicted with ailments that would have rendered their wild survival nearly impossible, including lesions, broken bones, and signs of infection. This indicates that whoever coexisted with these creatures took great time and care to ensure their safety and well-being, providing for them as they would a human friend or family member.

KING TUT'S DUCKS

Objectively the most famous mummy of ancient Egypt and arguably one of the most famous Egyptian archaeological discoveries of all time is none other than the young King Tutankhamun, frequently shortened to King Tut. The tomb he was discovered in has yielded a literal and figurative treasure trove of information for the world of Egyptology. While many have and could dedicate an entire book to the fascinating historic and scientific implications of this discovery, I obviously want to focus on something much less consequential. That, of course, being . . . the kid loved ducks!

Duck iconography is frequent in the tomb of the Golden King. One of several pairs of sandals found alongside him has the heads of ducks carved and displayed on them next to a lotus flower, like feathery guardians who guided his every step. Along with this there were earrings depicting ducks as well as wristbands, bracelets, and other items of jewelry and decorations. While many of the grave goods are decorated in regal splendor with gold, ivory, and jewels, the love the young man had for this wild animal transcends his royal blood.

Of all the discoveries that bear this same theme, there is one that stands out as particularly somber—a small tunic bearing once-colorful embroidery of the little king's favorite animal. While Tutankhamun was small for a nineteen-year-old at the time of his death, his tunic was smaller. Likely it was a childhood outfit that had been decorated with the artful hands of royal tailors to match the needs of an exuberant little boy. Despite having grown out of it long ago, it was found alongside childhood toys in the shape of ducks, in a chest decorated with the carved likenesses of ducks, in the tomb of a little boy who was born into royalty and who loved nothing more than the beating wings and feathered breasts of ducks.

RIP, RIP

When considering the menagerie of animals that humans have fawned over throughout time there are some obvious big players that come to mind. Cats and dogs, of course, and one could also argue for birds, fish, and the occasional snake. But what if I told you that for a moment in American history the most famous animal in the United States, and potentially the world, was none other than a Texas horned lizard?

Named after the fictitious Rip Van Winkle, the very non-fictitious Ol' Rip was a Texas horned lizard who rose to stardom in 1928. Originally this scaly fella was named Blinky and was owned by a young Texan named Will Wood (no relation). On July 31, 1897, Ernest, Will's father, took Blinky for an unscheduled visit to the Eastland, Texas courthouse, which was under construction at the time. It was here that this man decided to seal the lizard in the building's foundation with a copy of the Holy Bible.

Now you may be thinking to yourself: "What?"

And that's a very good question.

Horned lizards are known for a unique piece of biology. Due to living in an environment that is inhospitable on a good day, they have evolved the ability to become dormant under the right environmental pressures. Whether it's cold, drought, or lack of food, these bizarre creatures can slow their metabolic needs to a standstill, essentially walking the razor's edge between life and death until conditions improve. While this skill is most useful for getting through the winter, there is an old legend in the American West that they can survive in this state for one hundred years. Starting to see why a man buried his son's pet under a courthouse?

Thirty years after Blinky's entombment, a new courthouse was needed in the city of Eastland. As demolition on the old courthouse commenced, Ernest began to drum up hype for the reveal of "Schrödinger's horned lizard." On February 18, 1928, in front of an audience of several thousand people, including priests and armed guards, Blinky was removed from the cornerstone. To the shock and glee of the audience, he was alive!

After being renamed to Ol' Rip, word of this miraculous lizard spread fast. Flashbulbs blazed, creating this hilarious picture where the only person who appeared to feel any joy was the holder of the undead reptile. The *New York Times* published his name in their pages, he was sprinkled across the cover of *Science*, and local newspapers claimed him to be "the most famous animal since the serpent in the Garden of Eden!" News soon reached the President of the United States, and this miraculous horned lizard earned a visit from President Calvin Coolidge himself!

After eleven months in the limelight, the little critter took his leave to the great beyond. Croaked, if you will. He was given a hero's burial, embalmed in a custom-made glass and velvet casket that still resides in the "new" courthouse. His legacy has been carried on in Eastland with an Old Rip Day, a Rip Fest, and even a Rip Oath, which reads as a vow to "perpetuate the truth of Old Rip; so, help me God," and is one of the most Texas things I have ever read. Next time you need a reminder of the power of one, just remember that a horned lizard that was left for dead in a hole captured the eyes of an entire nation.

CHER AMI

A loud boom shattered the momentary silence. The ground shook as though the Earth itself was trying to fight back against those who walked on it. He let out a low coo and anxiously ruffled his wings in his little box as bits of dirt and stone pelted down around him like angry summer rain. While unsure of what exactly was going on, he knew it was bad. Very, very bad. The invisible string of instinct tugged at his chest again, calling him to spread his wings and fly home and away from whatever hell he was in. He squawked again, flapping his wings against the wooden sides of his cell, but to no avail.

Suddenly the door was ripped open and a man wearing leather gloves scooped him up from the inside of his cage. He was yelling something. Everyone was yelling something. The air itself seemed to be screaming. He wriggled against the vice-like grip of the man's hand

but couldn't free himself. Another man ran to him, hunched low with one hand on his helmet and the other clutching a small metal tube. Under a hail of machine-gun fire, the running man stopped short and handed the tube to the man with the leather gloves before returning to cover. He was lifted to eye level, and the gloved man began to tie the small canister to his little leg, cursing under his breath.

There was a pause in the din, as if the Earth had stopped for a breath. Through the silence came a whistle, causing everyone to look up, waiting to see if the cruel hand of fate had chosen them. Sure enough, the ground only a stone's throw away was ripped up with a sound that was deafening. The running man with the helmet, who had been just paces away, simply ceased to exist.

As the ringing in his ears faded, he realized they were on the ground, knocked flat by the blast. The man with the gloves had finished the knot and held his tiny body close. As if the bird was listening, the man whispered, "Save us, my dear friend," and flung him into the sky. His wings beat hard as he rose above the destruction below him. His tiny heart raced as he reached toward the treetops, whose leaves hung like tattered feathers. Above the smoke he could begin to see blue sky, clouds, and rolling fields scarred at the hands of his keepers.

There was a pop and a sting and he felt himself falling. Something was wrong but he couldn't tell what. The world began to fade as he tumbled from the sky, broken trees rising up to meet him like the limbs of a hungry Earth. As he spiraled, that pulling in his chest tugged at him again. His vision was returning—not well, but enough. The tug again. He knew he couldn't die here.

His wings kicked into action and corrected his spin toward the Earth, and with every fiber of strength he had, he began to gain altitude. Below him was a chorus of pops over a rhythmic cracking that disintegrated the branches around him. He pulled above the trees and the popping faded. He continued to fly higher and higher until the sound disappeared. Above him was a blue sky painted with white clouds, and below him were fields of green stained with black. As blood wept from his shattered leg and pierced breast, the tug kept him moving. And so he flew away from the chaos and to the safe haven to which his instincts drew him.

Many of you may be familiar with the Lost Battalion, a heroic group of American soldiers who found themselves trapped behind enemy lines during the War to End All Wars (otherwise known as World War I). They have been the subject of storytelling, film adaptations, and ballads sung by Swedish metal bands. But what seems to escape this story filled with the daring heroism and survival of mankind against all odds, is the fact that the Lost Battalion was saved by a pigeon.

On October 2, 1918, around 550 American soldiers became trapped behind enemy lines in the Argonne Forest in France. Rather than surrender, the men stood their ground, fighting relentlessly against the onslaught of German soldiers who surrounded them from all sides. Far out of range of radio communication, and with every messenger who tried to get help being captured or killed, Major Charles Whittlesey, leader of the battalion, had to find a new way to save his men. By October 4, the situation had devolved from bad to really bad. American artillery, unaware of the location of the lost battalion, began to shell their position, assuming it was under enemy control. In a desperate attempt to save his men, Whittlesey sent out carrier pigeons with messages attached to their legs to relay their distress to American headquarters. Many birds met their demise to German fire as the situation grew more and more desperate.

Finally, with few options left, Whittlesey prepared to send his last bird. A little fellow by the name of Cher Ami. He prepared a note to attach to the bird's leg that simply read:

"We are along the road parallel to 276.4.
Our own artillery is dropping a barrage directly on us.
For heaven's sake, stop it."

With the last-ditch plea for help attached, Cher Ami was released into the fray. Unaware of standard military tactics, as many pigeons tend to be, Cher Ami made a beeline for his roost at the US Military Headquarters, which happened to be directly through the German line as the crow (or in this case, pigeon) flies. The brave little bird was shot almost immediately after takeoff, piercing his chest, and causing him to fall to the ground within sight of the American troops. Yet somehow he managed to right himself, take flight, and continue through heavy fire from German guns and successfully arrive at the American headquarters 25 miles away. By the time he arrived he had been half blinded, shot through the chest and his right leg was held on by one resilient tendon.

Because of the fearlessness of this bird, the United States military redirected artillery to the German line and was able to relieve and ultimately rescue the otherwise doomed Lost Battalion. By the time they were rescued, their numbers had been decimated from 500 to around 190 men. A tragic and staggering loss of life that rightfully lives on through story and song. But the survival of those lucky few would not have been possible had it not been for the courage and bravery of a daring little bird.

Despite not being an enlisted man or a heroic general, Cher Ami was honored upon his return and death in the United States. Awarded the Croix de Guerre for his bravery, Cher Ami was memorialized with all the honors of any man who had selflessly served his country. In fact, his honors went even beyond that,

THE ENCYCLOPEDIA OF THE WEIRD AND WONDERFUL

being posthumously awarded one of the first Animals in War and Peace Medal of Bravery in 2019 at a ceremony in Washington, DC. Today, Cher Ami stands proudly on his one leg in a glass case at the Smithsonian Institution. A stoic reminder of the animals who fought alongside their human caretakers and those who sacrificed themselves so others may live.

FEATHERED FRIENDS

While Cher Ami is one of the few birds to be laid to rest with military honors, his is far from the only story of avian heroism from the Great War. One honorable mention goes to Pigeon No. 498. While underwhelmingly named, this bird found itself onboard the British vessel *Nelson* when it was engaged by a German U-boat. The *Nelson*, an auxiliary component of the British Navy, was vastly underequipped for the engagement, not only being outgunned by the U-boats' 88 mm cannon, but also not retrofitted with radio. Thomas Crisp, the skipper of the *Nelson*, released Pigeon No. 498 as the tide of battle turned against the British. The bird was able to make it back to shore and carry the message of the sinking, leading to the rescue of the six survivors, including Crisp's son, also named Thomas. Crisp, who was responsible for this rescue call, was not among them, having gone down with the ship.

These are just two of several stories of the some 250,000 pigeons that served in the Great War. They delivered countless messages, traveled incalculable miles, and carried both life and death on their delicate feathered wings.

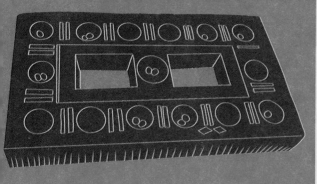

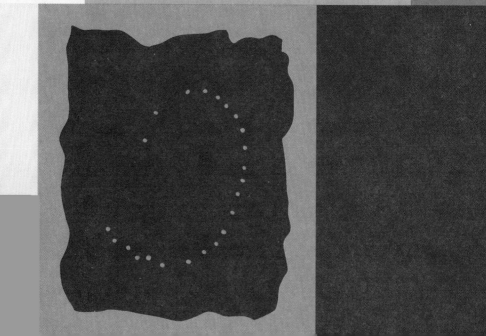

CHAPTER 4

PLAY AND LEISURE

✦ ✦ ✦

Leisure time is one of the longest-running traditions we have as humans. Since long before the capitalist machine managed to convince you that free time is a privilege, people have delighted in finding ways to entertain themselves when the day's work is done. Across time, our distant and recent ancestors invented myriad ways to keep themselves entertained in the workers' camps of ancient mines and the gilded palaces of royalty. Let's take a deeper look at the multitude of ways humanity has fought off our most wicked enemy: boredom.

DIVJE BABE FLUTE

The ability to play music is one of the most impressive things we have managed to develop and refine as a species. With its theorized humble beginnings as rhythm, produced on rudimentary percussion instruments, the art has expanded exponentially to the wide range of styles, sounds, and musical instruments that we have today. Our species has mastered this art for the simple reason that it makes us feel something: elation, grief, suspense, sorrow, hope, and everything in between.

Currently, the oldest-known musical instrument in the world is a small piece of cave bear bone held in the National Museum of Slovenia. Despite sustaining damage over the last sixty thousand years, the object is unmistakably an ancient flute. Bearing two currently preserved holes, as well as two that have widened due to large breakages in the instrument's surface, this device was created by none other than our ancient relatives, the Neanderthals.

The purpose of this small instrument is currently unknown, with some suggesting that it was used much like a duck call or some sort of animal lure. While that is possible, experimental archaeology that aimed to recreate and test the flute found that it had a two-and-a-half-octave range, more than enough to play essentially any modern piece of music. While it is likely that there was some utilitarian use for this painstakingly crafted piece of ancient bone, I believe it would be foolish to assume its use would end there. It seems likely to me that a tool like this would quickly become a staple of entertainment, as hunters who were used to using it by day as a tool returned to their camps at night and employed these budding skills to captivate their community by firelight. Perhaps somewhere, long ago, on this planet that was covered in glaciers and dark, untouched forests, the haunting tune of this ancient instrument wafted out of a cave into a dark and mysterious world that stretched in all directions to infinity.

FINDING ITS VOICE

The Divje Babe Flute was the subject of extensive study. The claim that this was potentially the oldest instrument ever discovered necessitated confirmation. To achieve this, the instrument was scanned, both inside and out, to create a render that could be recreated on a 3D printer. Using computer software, archaeologists were also able to recreate the missing pieces to create a reproduction of how the full instrument would have looked. Experimental archaeologists used bones of similar composition as well as stone tools akin to those found at the site in an attempt to recreate the instrument. Sure enough, this was not only possible with the tools at hand, but also created a fully functioning (if eerily haunting) instrument.

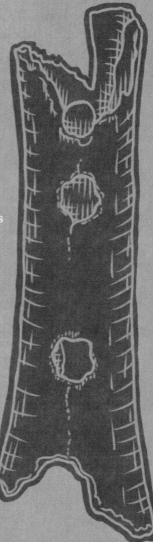

JUST A SHADOW ON THE WALL

The cave paintings of Pleistocene beasts are some of the most well-known examples of Paleolithic art in the entire world. While cave paintings can be found nearly everywhere on the planet, it is the works of the caves in Europe that have attracted a significant spotlight. Places like Lascaux Cave and Chauvet Cave (both in France) captivate visitors from around the world as we look back at the depictions of wild beasts that roamed the world nearly thirty thousand years ago. While archaeologists have always been stunned by these creations, recent analysis has found that they may have been far more advanced than we once thought.

Recent studies of cave paintings from France to Spain suggest that these cave paintings are merely half the story. When illuminated with firelight, the flickering light casts ever-shifting shadows on the walls that in some cases makes it appear as though the animals are moving. It suggests that ancient people deliberately painted their animal characters on uneven surfaces so that the flames of their hearths would essentially bring the animals to life. This is, in effect, the very oldest example we have of cinema.

This new understanding has helped researchers unlock a deeper understanding of some of the depictions, such as an eight-legged bison in the Chauvet Cave. Before the firelight discovery there was no real explanation for this beast's mutation, but with the addition of a flickering flame the creature comes to life as it seems to gallop across the wall.

This single discovery has shattered our understanding of these paintings. Going beyond hunters' instruction manuals or the results of boredom, these ancient paintings are multidimensional pieces of art that still function to this day. Tens of thousands of years before the

first film was made and modern cinema arose, people like you and me huddled around a campfire and watched in awe as the ghostly shadows brought the beasts of the outside world to life.

THE MYSTERIOUS SHELLFISH GAME

The archaeological site of Tlacuachero in modern-day Mexico centers around an enormous pile of discarded shells. In archaeological terms, a refuse pile such as this is referred to as a midden. This gigantic garbage pile was built up by the Paleo-Indigenous peoples of Central America about five thousand years ago. The pile that is made up mostly of bivalve shells from the surrounding mangrove forest also has several flattened clay floors.

ASK THE PAST

When analyzing history, especially that of Indigenous communities, it is always beneficial to analyze contextual documents. In the case of the Tlacuachero site's strange indentations, the 1907 book *Games of the North American Indians* by Stewart Culin helped researchers come to the board-game conclusion. While 1907 may seem outdated, it actually has information that's more pertinent to the ways of life for Indigenous populations that had consistent aspects for thousands of years before colonization. This book showed not only that many Indigenous groups participated in dice games and betting, but also that other layouts and boards resembled the ones found at this site. For this reason, it is always worth looking for sources like this one whenever you're trying to interpret a site.

These platforms show no evidence of constant habitation, rather acting as a work site for those preparing the fish and clams that would have been harvested at this site. But along with the post holes that once held fish drying racks, archaeologists found a series of strange carvings in the clay floors.

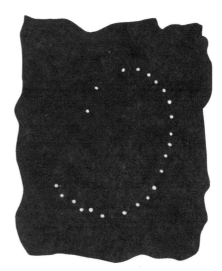

Consisting of twenty-four small holes in the clay aligned around a central rock depression in the shape of an oval, these patterns appear in multiple different spots all confined to the same area of the clay work platform. For much of the time that they have been known about it was assumed that they served a utilitarian purpose, in some way aiding fish and shellfish preparation. Beyond that, these patterns were assigned a punchline of archaeological diagnoses: ritual purposes. These two options leave out myriad other potential uses that hadn't even been explored.

Another option proposed by those working at the site is that these are the remains of some sort of ancient board game. This seems a potentially likely option as workers at the site would be inclined to find a way to relax during a day's work or between shipments of fish. Without homes or personal belongings at the site, it is possible that the fishermen had this permanent entertainment system installed to keep themselves busy in their free time.

THE ROYAL GAME OF UR

Hands down the most famous and influential ancient game is the Royal Game of Ur. Dating back nearly five thousand years, it was played by both royalty and common people alike. The first iterations of this game were found during the excavations of the ancient Sumerian city of Ur back in the early 1900s, and are beautiful examples of ancient craftsmanship.

The most stunning and recognizable of the five game boards discovered in the early excavations of the Royal Cemetery of Ur is composed of a wooden backing inlaid with shells, stones, and precious minerals. It is a beautiful creation that has somehow managed to withstand the test of time to share its secrets today. Ever since the discovery of the first board, countless examples of the Royal Game of Ur have been discovered across the Middle and Near East, including as far north as Cyprus and as far south as Sri Lanka. Talk about a realm of influence!

This game is believed to have been immensely popular, with versions of it found alongside the tomb of King Tutankhamun. It is theorized that as time went on, the Royal Game of Ur slowly morphed in form, in some areas inspiring new games and in others dying off altogether. However, among the Paradesi Jewish community in modern India, anthropologists found a traditional game that was functionally the exact same as the Royal Game of Ur, which was played as recently as the 1950s after at least five thousand years of existence. There is currently some speculation that it was this ancient game that went on to inspire backgammon, which is still popular today!

PLAYING THE ROYAL GAME OF UR

The Royal Game of Ur is deceptively simple and surprisingly fun. Just before sitting down to write this, I played an online version against a computer and lost horribly. I believe this is because the computer was cheating. Should you have a friend who would be interested in partaking in one of the oldest human traditions, here's how.

WHAT YOU WILL NEED

+ The game board (pictured on previous page).

+ Fourteen playing pieces (seven for each player)—these can be coins, bottle caps, or whatever else you have lying around.

+ Four four-sided dice! Traditionally four pyramidal dice with markings on two of each of their corners would be rolled. The sum of all the colored corners that pointed up would be the number of spaces moved. This meant that the highest number that could be rolled was four and the lowest was zero. You can also have four popsicle sticks with sides painted different colors to achieve roughly the same effect. If you are using a traditional six-sided dice you will have to reroll when you get a five or a six.

+ A good attitude.

UNDERSTANDING THE BOARD

+ The Royal Game of Ur is divided into twenty squares. There is a central lane that divides the board in half. On either side of this center track are the sides of each team, consisting of the four-tile start and the two-tile end. Players begin by navigating up their four-tile start to the beginning of the central path,

THE ENCYCLOPEDIA OF THE WEIRD AND WONDERFUL

then down the center to their two-tile exits. The objective of the game is to navigate all seven of your pieces through your starting section, down the shared middle track, and out the other end before your opponent.

✦ There are several tiles that have rosettes on them. These are some of the most important points in the game. Landing one of your pieces on these tiles not only allows you to roll the dice again, but also makes that piece invulnerable to your opponent for as long as it occupies this spot. This makes the central rosette the most important position in the entire game.

✦ Don't go down your opponent's side. Your only shared territory is the center.

HOW TO PLAY

✦ The youngest player rolls the dice first.

✦ Your pieces may be moved by the amount that is indicated on the dice.

✦ You may have as many pieces on the board at a time as you would like.

✦ Pieces may NOT occupy the same tile.

✦ BUT if you land on the same square as an opponent's piece in the central section (except for the rosette) you bump your opponent back to the start. Sorry!

✦ To successfully get your piece off the board and earn a point, you must roll the exact amount needed to take one extra move off of the last tile. If you are on the last tile on the board and roll a four, that sucks for you.

The interpretation of this board game is largely thanks to the work of philologist Irving Finkel, an inspirational wizard of a man who deciphered the texts explaining the rules of this game. If you are so inclined, I highly recommend you watch his videos online of him playing it, as he is truly one of the great characters of archaeology.

THE MANY MANCALAS

Many people have played mancala in their lifetime, the classic board game that many grew up playing after being told that it is an "ancient Egyptian game." Play involves moving colored stones across a wooden board in an attempt to hoard all the playing pieces to yourself. While it is true that the ancient Egyptians did possess a mancala game that is quite similar to what we play today, the name we use for this game is a classification of a whole litany of traditional board games played across Africa and the Near East.

The mancala game family is defined by the play style and layout. All of these games involve a board or surface with cup-like depressions, stones, beans, or clay pieces to be used for play, and a cyclical around-the-board nature. Today there are countless versions of this simple yet highly replayable game structure found throughout the world. There is the game of Bao, which comes from what are now the modern countries of Tanzania and Kenya, and whose name translates to "wood" in the Swahili language. The Konso people of Central

Ethiopia have Lamlameta, traditionally played on wooden boards with seeds as playing pieces. In southern India there is Pallanguzhi, which is played as far away as Sri Lanka and Malaysia. And in the Dominican Republic there is Hoyito, a similar game whose board is often carved into the dirt.

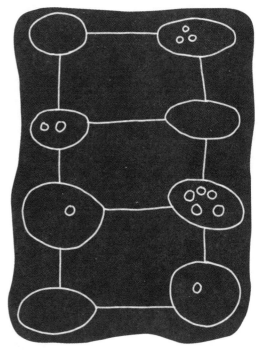

The influence and simplicity of the core of this game type allowed it to have a huge sphere of influence throughout time, splintering off to create the vast amounts of cultural differences in its play style that can still be seen across the world. It's fascinating to think about how this tradition began, what the first boards may have looked like, and who were the first to play them.

STICKBALL

The ancient game of stickball has become one of the most popular games played in North America now. Since its inception, the game has morphed as equipment and players have changed and improved, yet its core is still much the same as it has been for hundreds, if not thousands, of years. Today this highly popular sport is more commonly known under its modern name: lacrosse.

The game we now call lacrosse was invented by the Algonquin peoples of the northeastern part of what is now called the United

States. Indigenous oral tradition claims that this ancient game was gifted to the people by the Creator as a form of entertainment as well as healing. Because of this, it was a crucial intercommunity event that fostered celebrations, feasts, and plenty of betting. Large games held in the springtime would see the participation of men from the age of ten and younger all the way up to men in their seventies and eighties who had the energy to get in on the action. Traditionally referred to as stickball, it was played with sticks that eventually became netted with deer sinew and a ball that was either made of wood or animal hide. The game involved transporting the ball from one side of the play area to the other and had essentially one rule: the players may never touch the ball. And the Algonquins took this sport seriously, making today's version look like child's play.

Stickball games were a spectacular event where multiple individual tribes, settlements, and groups would come together to compete in the games. The play area between the goal posts was between a couple hundred yards (modern lacrosse is played on a 110-yard, or 101 m, soccer pitch) and literal miles. This meant that the play areas were absolutely enormous, and when paired with the informal "there are no boundaries" rule, players were left to essentially travel however far they needed to secure a point. Today a lacrosse team is made up of ten players, but to account for this practically limitless play space, the Algonquins could have from a hundred to literal thousands of players active on the field at once. The sheer scale of these games meant that they could stretch on for days.

Missionaries who first encountered Indigenous populations playing this game in the 1600s wrote the name down as Lacrosse, and in the years since the name has stuck. It is still an immensely popular game in the United States and has been covered with more specialized equipment and rules than one could count. But it is always worth remembering that the true origins of this game did not include plastic face masks and Astroturf, but in the rolling hills of a continent blanketed in ancient forests and sweeping prairies from sea to shining sea.

THE LONE BOARD GAME

The island of Aotearoa, home to the Māori people, is one of the last places on Earth to experience the presence of humans. While current evidence suggests that the ancestors of the Māori people only arrived on this island around one thousand years ago, the groups that live there have developed a rich and thriving culture. Yet this island, currently known as New Zealand, has only one traditional board game, known as Mū tōrere.

It would probably be safer to say that New Zealand only has one *surviving* board game, but regardless Mū tōrere is a unique Māori

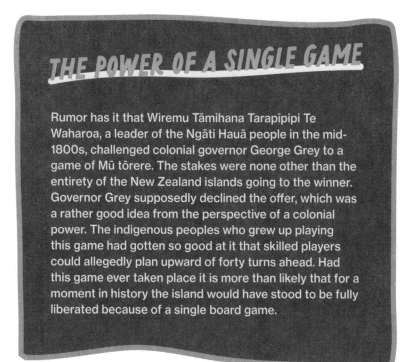

THE POWER OF A SINGLE GAME

Rumor has it that Wiremu Tāmihana Tarapipipi Te Waharoa, a leader of the Ngāti Hauā people in the mid-1800s, challenged colonial governor George Grey to a game of Mū tōrere. The stakes were none other than the entirety of the New Zealand islands going to the winner. Governor Grey supposedly declined the offer, which was a rather good idea from the perspective of a colonial power. The indigenous peoples who grew up playing this game had gotten so good at it that skilled players could allegedly plan upward of forty turns ahead. Had this game ever taken place it is more than likely that for a moment in history the island would have stood to be fully liberated because of a single board game.

THE ENCYCLOPEDIA OF THE WEIRD AND WONDERFUL

creation that is still played. The game is closely associated with the Ngāti Porou people of the East Cape region of the North Island. The game itself is simple in rules and moves, but the strategy behind it can be taken *very* seriously.

The game board consists of eight spaces in a circle around the center spaces, traditionally created either on the ground or on a piece of tree bark stretched between sticks. Each player receives four pieces that fill all eight spots on the outside, leaving the center open. Without jumping over other pieces, the players then take turns moving their pieces to the ever-shifting central spot on the board in an attempt to leave their opponent with no move to make. Think of it like a giant game of tic-tac-toe, but you actually have to strategize instead of just taking the central spot and guaranteeing a draw.

Europeans who colonized the islands first theorized that the game was derived from their game of draughts or checkers. Though it may have come as a shock, the Europeans learned that not everything on Earth was inspired by them and that this game has been a staple for the Aotearoa Islanders for countless years.

LIFE IN STEREOSCOPE

You may have grown up with a toy resembling a red plastic box in which one could insert a wheel containing images of dinosaurs, cityscapes, trucks, and other heavy machinery. Upon looking into the lenses of this device, the viewer would be delighted with a perceived three-dimensional space that appeared to bring the little slides to life.

STEREOSCOPY REPEATS ITSELF

There is a clear connection to be made between stereoscope technology and the advancements of the modern world. While it may seem like a stretch, I assure you it is reasonable to say that this piece of entertainment was the precursor, or even roundabout inspiration, for modern virtual reality (VR) technology. While vastly different in complexity, both immerse a viewer in a different world. While today's VR is a clunky and budding technology, it is likely that if you read this just a handful of years down the road, it will be unrecognizable from reality as I write this. Whatever it looks like in your world now, think of how far we have come; from the humble wooden stereoscope that gained its capabilities from a natural optical phenomenon to the sleek, highly sophisticated headset or goggles that you have now.

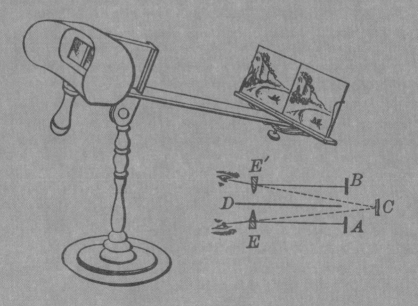

Branded as a View-Master, this little device is the most recent iteration of a long-running type of entertainment technology: the stereoscope.

In 1838, Charles Wheatstone stumbled across an unusual optical phenomenon. He found that if one were to view two images of the same subject but depicted at slightly different angles, the ever-impressive human brain would stitch the images together and create a three-dimensional shape. This discovery unlocked a world of potential. While the concept had originally been pioneered with drawings, the refinement of the newly invented photograph skyrocketed the popularity of this invention. It wasn't long before the technology had been refined enough that it was on the market for all to enjoy. And enjoy it they did.

With the craze for stereoscopes fueled by companies such as the London Stereoscopic Company in England and Underwood & Underwood in the United States, popularity for these new pieces of technology boomed. The London Stereoscopic Company had over twenty-five thousand images a day and sold over three million handheld stereoscopes between the 1860s and 1920s. The relative affordability and sheer diversity of available images made it a peak of personal entertainment.

Stereoscope slides were sold in sets with a thematic connection but could also be bought individually. These images covered just about everything you could imagine, being similar to a nineteenth-century Google Images. You could get your hands on pictures of landscapes and national parks, city streets, historic towns, excavations of ancient ruins, parties and traditions, comedy, pornography, royalty, and just about everything in between. While it may seem antiquated to us today, the ability to look into a box and see a scene come to life in three dimensions was groundbreaking at the time, with people like Queen Victoria herself being captivated by the little device at the 1851 Crystal Palace Exhibition in London.

THE MOST POPULAR GAME
IN THE WORLD

Humanity has found millions of unique ways to entertain ourselves through time, but there is one single piece of entertainment that is likely one of the most-consumed in the entirety of human existence. It arose fairly recently in the grand scheme of things, and yet has become a phenomenon unlike anything else. It is none other than Tetris.

The game that we all know and love as Tetris began in the current Russian capital of Moscow. Its creator, Alexey Pajitnov, developed the first iteration of this game in 1984. He drew inspiration from pentominoes, a game he had played as a child that involved interlocking pieces like those in Tetris. Development took place on the Soviet-produced computer called the Electronica 60, which by today's standards was essentially as powerful as a pocket calculator with no batteries. Yet Pajitnov managed to use it to create the single most sold piece of gaming entertainment in the entire world to date. In fact, because of its popularity, I don't even think there is really a reason for me to go through the effort of writing down how it's played. It's Tetris. I promise you are familiar with it.

But what you may not be as familiar with is the quantifiable popularity of this smash-hit piece of entertainment. Since its creation, Tetris has sold nearly 550 million copies. To put this into perspective, the second-most-sold game, Minecraft, has sold nearly *half* that number.

While it may seem odd to include a piece about a video game in this book, it is important to note how much this single game changed the course of entertainment. Tetris helped fan the flames of the Nintendo Game Boy, which sold 35 million copies and generated an *insane* amount of capital. It was one of the first widely available "home-brewed" games that helped inspire countless others to go on to make their own games, eventually transitioning the industry to include more console and home games alongside the arcade games that ruled the early 1980s. The release of the game to the rest of the world outside the Soviet Union in 1987 was also a turning point in the relations between the Soviet Union and the United States, two countries that had found themselves locked in the Cold War.

It is impossible to quantify the amount of people who were so inspired by it that they went on to study computers, game design, or electronic arts. While it is a small moment in history, it is truly incredible how different the world may have been without this one simple game designed by a man who was inspired by one of his favorite childhood games.

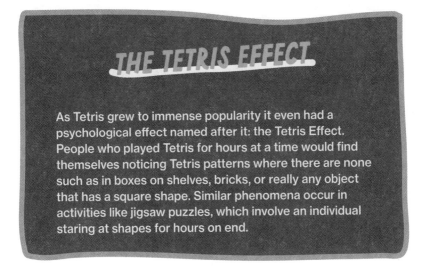

THE TETRIS EFFECT

As Tetris grew to immense popularity it even had a psychological effect named after it: the Tetris Effect. People who played Tetris for hours at a time would find themselves noticing Tetris patterns where there are none such as in boxes on shelves, bricks, or really any object that has a square shape. Similar phenomena occur in activities like jigsaw puzzles, which involve an individual staring at shapes for hours on end.

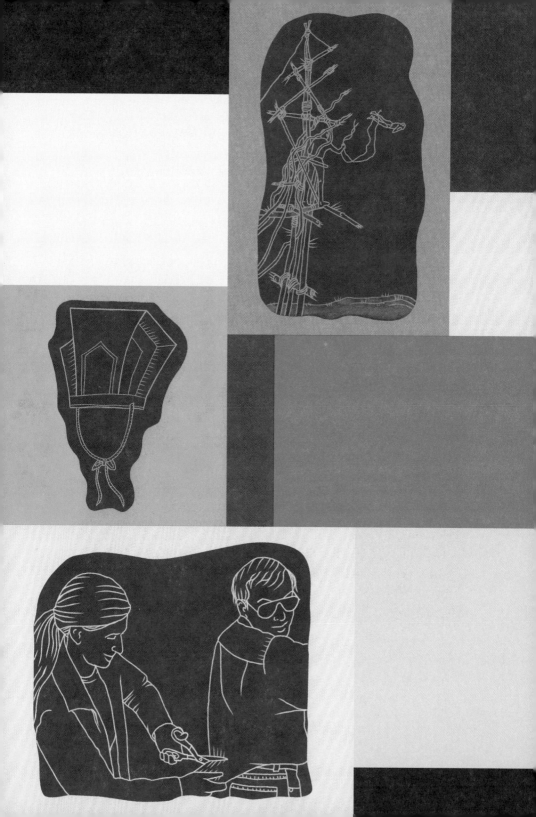

CHAPTER 5
RITES AND RITUALS

✦ ✦ ✦

Our species is on a constant journey to prove itself. Whether to each other, ourselves, or a higher power, we work ceaselessly to show the world that we have got what it takes. The idea of a rite of passage is an ancient one, and one that has countless definitions. It can be the transition from a child to an adult, from an apprentice to a master, or from a humble believer to being one with God. But because of the nearly limitless applicability of these rituals of passage, we as a species have developed transitions and pivotal points that are worth celebrating.

WALKABOUT

One rite of passage from the First Nations peoples of Australia dates back eternally and has been widely misunderstood by the recent non-indigenous inhabitants of the continent. The tradition is known as a walkabout but has also been referred to as "temporary mobility" in recent years, due to the former term having a negative connotation in modern Australia.

In First Nations culture, when a boy reaches the age of adolescence he is deemed ready to depart on this journey of self-discovery. The practice involves the young man leaving his community to explore the countryside for months at a time. The traveler would spend the duration of their journey living off the land. Because of the challenging nature of this journey, it was at the discretion of the community elders to determine whether the youngster was ready to embark on such a trip. In preparation, other members of the community would help teach the young adventurer the skills needed to survive—everything from hunting and identifying medicinal plants to navigation. Only those who were deemed fit both physically and mentally would be allowed to proceed.

The traditional walkabout was more than just a test of survival and fitness, as it was primarily a journey of self-discovery. Those who undertook this feat would frequently be initiated in some way, such as a new piercing or having a tooth removed. Along the way, the traveler would face the ultimate challenge of being alone with oneself and one's thoughts. This helped teach the primary lesson of the walkabout: self-understanding. With months spent alone, young men were expected to return from their journey with a greater sense of self and a deeper understanding of the world around them.

UPANAYANA

Rites of passage are commonplace in many religious circles. Traditions like these have developed over hundreds if not thousands of years and can act as a symbolic transition into adulthood, a member of the religious community, or between different chapters of one's life. Modern Hindu communities in India have just such a practice, which is known as *upanayana*. The ritual symbolizes a young man's "second birth," which sees him given the respects and privileges of acceptance into his social class. To symbolize this rebirth, some who participate in this ceremony are given a new spiritual name afterward.

The name *upanayana* translates to "sitting nearby," as much of the ceremony is conducted under the watchful eye of a teacher of spiritualism, referred to as a guru. It is typically performed with young men frequently around six or seven years of age, but their age can range up into their early twenties. Throughout the course of this rite of passage, the young man will be bathed, be given fresh clothes, and have his head shaved. Most importantly, however, is the gifting of their *janeu*. Also referred to as the sacred thread, the *janeu* is an item that the young man will frequently wear for the rest of his life. It is a long piece of woven cotton cordage consisting of three threads, which symbolize knowledge (*saraswati*), strength (*parvati*) and wealth (*lakshmi*). Typically, the sacred thread is worn over the left shoulder and slung down to the right hip, but there are many ways that people choose to wear them—some in a necklace fashion, others around their wrists or ankles.

With their new sacred thread in hand, young men will proceed forward as fully initiated members of their community. Frequently they will wear this thread their entire life, though they may occasionally switch it out for a new one. From this point, the initiated will hold the thread around their right thumb while reciting the Gayatri Mantra from the *Rig Veda* three times a day as they enter into their adult lives.

NANGGOL

The idea of danger is something that is common in many rites of passage. There is something about the thrill of walking the razor's edge between glorious victory and crushing defeat that makes such traditions as important as they are. While failure in some rites may run the risk of public ridicule or simply having to retry, there are others where poor execution can mean nothing short of death. Just one of these traditions can be found on the island nation of Vanuatu, in the South Pacific. On the island of Pentecost, one of around eighty islands that make up the nation, the indigenous peoples have a long-running and death-defying tradition referred to in the traditional Sa language as *nanggol*.

Known contemporarily as "land diving," the tradition involves the men of the community leaping headfirst from wooden towers to the ground below with nothing but vines tied to their ankles. These towers, called nanggol, can soar up to 100 feet (30 m), meaning that jumpers can descend at speeds of up to 45 miles per hour (72 km/h) before the elasticity of the vines (hopefully) breaks their fall just as their shoulders scrape the ground. The inclusion of "hopefully" here is important, as the margin of error in this ritual is slim. A failed attempt from this height, whether it be a miscalculation of vine length or simply bad luck, would be almost certainly fatal. For this reason, it is customary for all jumpers to settle any outstanding matters beforehand on the off chance they don't survive. The significance of this tradition pertains to yams, a crucial food source for the islanders. It is believed that the man who completes the highest jump successfully will be rewarded with the highest-yielding crop of yams.

The tradition is steeped in significance. The building of the tower itself is done by men who briefly remove themselves from the community, purify themselves, and remain abstinent until the construction is complete. The night before the ceremony, the builders sleep around the foot of the structure, are anointed with coconut oil, and are decorated with the tusks of wild boars in the morning before the celebration begins. Along with the men, there is also a smaller tower from which boys jump, symbolizing their induction into the ranks of men in the community.

THE ENCYCLOPEDIA OF THE WEIRD AND WONDERFUL

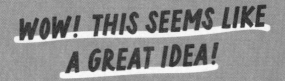

WOW! THIS SEEMS LIKE A GREAT IDEA!

You may have noticed that this tradition is eerily similar to the modern sport of bungee jumping. Well, that would be because it was the nanggol tradition that inspired a certain Mr. Hackett to modernize the tradition and turn it into an extreme sport. The New Zealander saw the tradition on a visit to the island in 1986 and just a year later completed the first successful bungee jump from the top of the Eiffel Tower. Despite the safety measures present in the modern sport, traditional practitioners shun these alterations in favor of their traditional, and way more hardcore, methods.

THE SUNRISE CEREMONY

For many cultures around the world, a young woman's first period is an important symbolic and physical initiation into womanhood. While in the modern world public discussion around this topic is scant at best, it remains one of the few concrete metrics by which many denote the transition from childhood to early adulthood. Because of this, many cultures have found their own ways to celebrate this massive milestone. One of these is the Sunrise Ceremony, which is practiced by the Apache people of the American Southwest.

Traditionally referred to as Na'ii'ees, the ceremony occurs after a young woman's first menstruation. The ensuing celebration has parts that span over the course of four days and involves ceremonies that symbolically represent the Apache origin myth. The young woman is meant to find her roots with Esdzanadehe, the first woman, and in doing so become more in touch with her early womanhood. The ceremony involves colorfully beaded and symbolically inspired outfits as well as singing and dancing and being painted with a pollen mixture.

In the days following the ceremony, it is said that the young woman is the closest she can be to the power of the first woman. During the four days immediately after the ceremony, she is not allowed to touch her own skin and must rely on the help of family to wash herself. Along with this she may not drink anything other than through a drinking tube that has been provided to her. However, during these days it is said that she has the power to cause rain showers as well as heal others with a simple touch. This tradition is still practiced today. While holding this event is difficult in the modern world due to its expense, it is still a vital part of modern Apache cultural heritage because of the celebration's complexity.

ULWALUKO

In the modern world one of the most common rites of passage for men is circumcision. This can be undertaken for religious purposes, as in the case of members of the Orthodox Jewish community, or simply societal purposes, as in the United States where around 70 percent of the male population has undergone the procedure. Regardless of one's personal opinions on it, this process is one that has thousands of years of history and bears an important significance in many cultures around the world. Just one of these is the ceremony known as *ulwaluko* by the Xhosa people of Southern Africa.

While many modern circumcisions are performed at birth, this tradition is meant to signify the transition from boyhood to manhood, and until the process is complete, a young man will not be recognized as an adult in the community. The ritualistic circumcision can happen as early as the age of thirteen.

To begin, the initiate has their face painted white with chalk and has the hair on their head shaved off. The circumcision procedure then takes place; in itself this is not pleasant, as it is traditionally performed without anesthetic or any sort of medical equipment beyond a blade. As a result, the procedure can have mixed effects on the young man.

Those who manage to walk away from the process spend anywhere from one to two months alone before reentering the community as a man. However, some procedures are not so successful. Botched cases have resulted in the necessity for genital amputation and, in even worse cases, death. It is estimated that 945 initiates died due to this procedure in the twenty years between 1995 and 2015. It is a difficult subject, and one where the utmost sensitivity must be taken in weighing the harsh reality that this dangerous practice is one of extreme cultural connotation. While strides have been made to at least make the process safer for initiates, many practitioners prefer the old methods and deem the modern approaches as not having the same significance.

THIS IS SPARTA?

Many of you may be familiar with the ancient Greek state of Sparta. In modern days, it has become the stuff of legends in both book and film, which have depicted the legendary and quasi-mythical last stand of the three hundred. But whether it's in a history book or a homoerotic Hollywood movie, there is one piece of Spartan life that frequently gets an offhand mention: the practice of systematic infanticide. Grim though it may be, this was undoubtedly a rite of passage that altered the face of this ancient state. For much of history, historians have debated whether or not the Spartans partook in this barbaric practice. With no current physical evidence found to substantiate either theory, anthropologists must rely on primary sources and other writings to piece together this dark chapter of Greek history.

The main source from which these writings come is that of Plutarch, a Greek philosopher and historian who lived around 75 CE. In his works, Plutarch describes the Spartan practice of infanticide as one where infants were inspected by a panel of elders who determined whether or not they would be permitted to live or be sent to their death. The work describes sickly, misshapen, or otherwise undesirable infants being sent away to a "pit-like place on Mount Apothetal." This ruthless practice would have been one that ensured only strong children survived to carry on the Spartan cause, effectively casting off early on those who would become a "burden on society."

BARBARISM IS LEARNED

Across the Greek peninsula there have been many examples of infants with mild to serious birth defects that show evidence of having been cared for until their deaths, ranging from the mild, like a cleft palate, to the more severe, like hydrocephalus. There are even records of a Spartan king who was said to be far shorter than average and was "impaired in the legs," and yet he still went on to lead this nation of supposed eugenicists.

It is important to note that absence of evidence is not evidence of absence. There may very well have been cases, whether instructed by the state or the individual, of disabled infants being left to the mercy of exposure. However, we have to remind ourselves that barbarism is a learned trait, and the hate and viciousness that motivates such acts is vastly outweighed by the love and compassion that each of our ancestors carried within them, allowing us to still exist today.

The story of Spartan infanticide is still up for debate amongst scholars and historians, but that doesn't mean that its effect in the real world hasn't been felt. With an example of an ancient and stereotypically strong nation supposedly practicing this act, many leaders in the modern world have cited it as a supporting argument for eugenics. Most famously, the stories of Spartan infanticide were touted by Adolf Hitler as a supporting argument for the systematic extermination of those he deemed "inferior."

As you won't be surprised to know, modern archaeologists and historians debate this theory heavily. This primary source documenting the Spartans' cruelty was penned nearly eight hundred years after these events would have taken place. In this span of time it is more than likely that the story was embellished, altered, or made up altogether. Like all sciences, history is based on evidence, and while stories can contain evidence, there has yet to be any concrete proof of this supposed Spartan barbarism. In fact, there have been discoveries of the opposite.

WHITE SAGE

As we have seen so far, there are many different types of rites of passage practiced by many different groups. However, one running theme that you may have noticed is that many of these traditions are specific to a group of people—whether it be a religion, nation, or indigenous group. While many of these traditions are still practiced within these "in" groups, outsiders have a nasty habit of taking sacred aspects of many of these traditions, removing them from their context, and practicing them themselves. Nowhere is this more prevalent in my observations than that of Indigenous American traditions.

One example I have seen personally is the sale, purchase, and use of white sage. This plant is sold in a small bundle which is burned to create an aromatic smoke. This is used to both purify and cleanse people and places and is a sacred piece of traditional medicine for many Indigenous American communities. However, recently, and like all things, it has been commodified and sold to the biggest audience possible: white people. White sage can be found in grocery stores, yoga studios, and even superstores like Target and Walmart—all places where it shouldn't be. To put this into perspective, imagine you grew up in a Catholic family and went overseas to see Communion wafers for sale in a bulk bag in a superstore right next to a flight of

Communion wine in plastic nips (or shooters, depending on your local vernacular). Does reading the instructions on the back of the bag make someone who isn't Catholic qualified to partake in your practice? I would say likely not. Yet despite sage smudging being regarded as a closed practice by some and a restricted practice by many, it has become a staple of modern plastic spirituality.

As a result, the harvesting and sale of sage has caused a massive spike in demand from these outside communities. This has led white sage to be decimated in its wild range in what is now today known as California, as ton after ton of it is poached to supply the market. Related to this is the fact that part of what makes the sage burning ceremony so sacred is the fact that the sage is gathered with intent and respect, something that doesn't happen when it is poached for massive sale. Imagine if our hypothetical Communion wafers had a label on the back telling you that they were sourced by being stolen from a church storage room by the box so they could be sold at such a cheap price. Pretty scummy stuff.

You have probably seen these practices on TikTok, YouTube, or other social media platforms, where a person of non-Indigenous descent will perform a saging ceremony in their home that looks like an Ikea cross-pollinated with a Crate & Barrel. Remember that this is a bastardization of a sacred and spiritually nuanced ceremony, and not a representation of how it is practiced. It's like someone wearing a rosary because "it just looks so good for this Instagram picture."

GUAN LI

Many rites of passage and the ceremonies that go with them change over time. Perhaps customs change, or a colonial or invading presence alters the social status quo, or simply traditions are modified to make them more applicable in the present day. The Confucian coming-of-age ceremony known as Guan Li is just one of these rites.

Originally, this Han Chinese ceremony was practiced between the sexes at different points. Young men would be initiated to manhood at the age of twenty and young women into womanhood at the age of fifteen. While the ceremony is widely referred to as Guan Li ("headpiece ceremony") as a whole, the young women's ceremony was more specifically called Ji Li ("hairpin ceremony"). Today, the tradition takes place for both boys and girls between the ages of eighteen to twenty.

In this ceremony, headpieces and hairpins are placed on the heads of boys and girls respectively to denote their transition from childhood to adulthood. The entire operation is conducted by a teacher who delivers a speech to the young adults and their parents, who are also in attendance. The presence of this parental body is important for the celebration itself because the children must give thanks to them, as it is by their hands that they have been able to make it to this crucial moment.

This tradition shrunk in practice throughout China during the onslaught of Westernization. However, there are many within the Han Chinese community who have worked to get more in touch with this traditional practice and keep it alive for generations to come.

A TALE OF TAILS

While we have explored rites of passage within religious groups, ethnic communities, and cultures, these are far from the only groups in which people find themselves. In our modern and globalized world, many professions and hobbies have communities that are diverse in background and united by their shared passion, skill, or job. In the field of aviation, there is one rite of passage that stands to commemorate a new pilot's first major achievement: their first solo flight. It is one that is signified in an unusual way—by cutting off the pilot's shirt tails.

The origins of this tradition date back to the days long before radio communication. Rather than being wired to an air traffic control tower or to an instructor, aviation students had to heed the instruction of a teacher who sat behind them in the cockpit. In early aircraft, the noise of the engine and the wind would have been deafening, and without headphones instructors had to find a different way to instruct their understudies. To work around this, teachers would pull on the shirt tails of their students so that they could get the pilots' attention in order to administer instructions and tips.

Throughout their logged aerial hours, student pilots would experience quite a bit of shirt-tugging at the hands of their maestro, and because of this close bond, it became commonplace for students to have their shirt tails cut off by their instructor after completing their first solo flight. This symbolic gesture showed that the young pilot had the confidence of their peers and was ready to take to the skies without a need for backseat driving.

Today, this tradition that is as old as aviation itself is alive and well, with many flight academies continuing to perform this commemorative act. Since modern fashions no longer have shirt tails, the backs of tee shirts are often now the casualties instead. Inducted pilots may decorate their shirt backs with things such as the runway they landed on, personal mottos, names, jokes, or anything else they deem significant enough to adorn this personal symbol of success. Some training schools pin up these "shirt tails" as a bit of a permanent installation, as a dedication to all those who took to the skies and completed their very first solo flight.

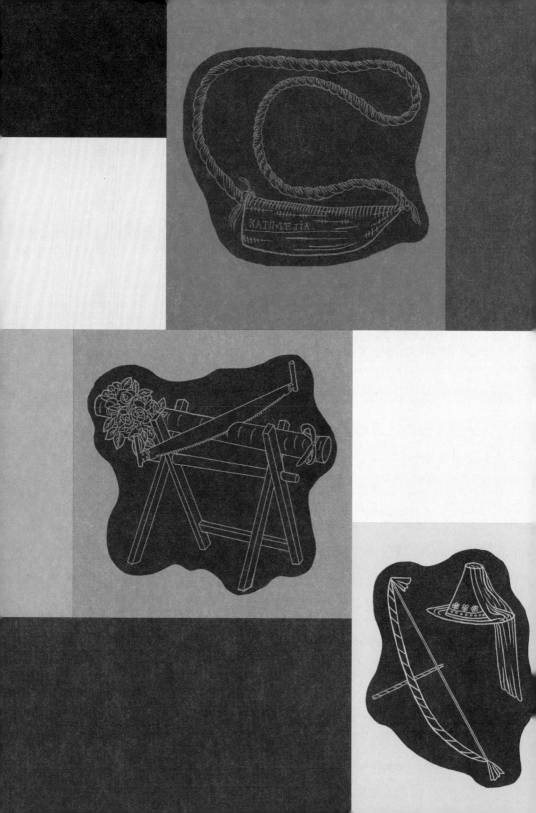

CHAPTER 6
LOVE AND SEXUALITY

Of all the things that make humanity unique, possibly our greatest trait is our immense ability to express love. Throughout time, every culture around the world has found the means to explain, define, and compartmentalize the countless ways we feel affection, attraction, and desire. In a world whose chapters are too often defined by hate, it is important to underscore the trait that makes us human: our ceaseless capacity to love.

FOURTH FINGER ON THE LEFT

Chances are many of the people you have interacted with today have a band on the fourth finger on their left hand. Perhaps you may even have one, in which case, congratulations! (Or two, if you practice stacking wedding and engagement bands.) The practice of displaying the commitment between two people through a wedding band is one that has persisted through all of recent memory and is one of the most universal symbols of the bond between a couple, but how did it begin? Well, you came to the right place.

Initially this tradition can be found in ancient Egypt as far back as six thousand years ago, though it is entirely possible that it dates back much further than that. The Egyptian bands were stylistically not all that similar to those we wear today, being made of anything from dried grasses and reeds to leather. The circular nature of the band was symbolically important as it was seen as an endless shape—one that had no beginning and no end—thus symbolizing the enduring bond of partnership. This shape also had a functional purpose, in that it would fall off your finger if it wasn't shaped like this. At the time, it was believed that the "ring finger" had a vein that ran directly to your heart, making it the obvious placement for the band. While we now know this fact to not be anatomically true, it is what anatomists like to call "really goddamn cute."

Like many great ideas, the Romans copied this tradition from the Egyptians and added their own flair, making rings from things like ivory, glass, and the now standard precious metals. By the Middle Ages, Christians began to further co-opt these heathen traditions and incorporated wedding bands into their marriage ceremonies. It was at this point that the rings began to branch out in style, to include written inscriptions, gemstones, and the highly popular motif of two hands clasped together, the last of which is exemplified in the Celtic claddagh ring. Christian churches from the Middle Ages, which were not known for their appreciation of fun, condemned these glamorous rings, and insisted the bands remain plain. While many today often go all out on a spectacular engagement ring, it is this medieval tradition that inspired the simple wedding bands that are most common today.

DOWRY ABOUT IT

Most of us are familiar with the concept of a dowry. Whether in the form of money, property, or physical assets, a dowry is a payment bestowed by a family to their daughter's groom. In the modern world this practice has widely fallen out of fashion, as its ethical context makes a wedding seem more like a business transaction than a celebration of love, potentially causing confusion and discomfort as it seems to place women on a par with property as a commodity to be traded. Through a contemporary lens this assumption may be valid, but it is equally true that, historically, in large and more densely populated civilizations, weddings *were* a form of trade, by which both families agreed to combine assets.

So, how does a dowry work? For this example, we will say that a dowry comes in the form of 300 acres (1.2 m^2) of land and a box of iron bars. Upon a woman's marriage after approval by her parents, both the land and the metal would be gifted to the new bride and groom. If the two were to split up, the dowry would default back to the bride's family. This meant that the husband may only have access to the dowry so long as the relationship remains. For this reason, it also acted as protection for the bride and peace of mind for her family, ensuring that the man she was with would treat her well and was willing to bear the responsibility of the dowry that, with a misstep, he would lose. Now, in our scenario things work out well. The two get on swimmingly, and this humble gift of land and iron, which he would *not* have exclusive jurisdiction over, would help with starting a life together, much in the same way that wedding gifts today aim to be functional ways to get young families on their feet. Beyond this, the dowry also works to solidify a strong bond between the bride's and groom's families.

The oldest examples of dowries come from the Code of Hammurabi, from around 2000 BCE, and can be found from this point on across the whole world—from Europe, to Africa, to Asia. Frequently, these transactions took the form of either land, livestock, or precious metals or gems. In European examples, the marriage of Louis VII to Eleanor of Aquitaine in 1137 granted him access to her dowry which was, of course, the region of Aquitaine. And thusly with the annulment of their marriage in 1152, all of Aquitaine was given back to Eleanor, its rightful owner.

PRE-COLUMBIAN "MARRIAGE"?

Being highly social creatures, every society that humankind developed has had some form of institution that could be broadly defined under the modern umbrella term of "marriage." While today that word carries with it the implication that it is a ceremony involving two individuals, legal contracts, and the intertwining of both people's financial and material lives, this is a highly modern and anglicized concept that would be alien to nearly everyone who lived before us. For example, Indigenous cultures in North America had their own systems of presenting their love that focused more on the benefits to one another and their community than the modern concept that is inseparably tied to the idea of ownership of both property and assets as well as children and even one's partner. An interesting example within the Pawnee people was the practice of having post-pubescent boys taught the ropes of "husband-hood" by their uncle's wife. This would resemble being a "husband understudy," where the young man would learn about providing for a family and working alongside a family unit.

Many Indigenous groups throughout pre-Columbian North America did not have an official wedding ceremony as we do today. This is rooted in the fact that many Indigenous cultures did not practice the European style of monogamous, legally declared love that we have grown accustomed to. One of the first major differences is that many Indigenous cultures viewed sex as separate to marriage. While it certainly is a bond that develops and fosters a prolonged partnership, the idea of sex being confined to marriage only came after the enforcement of Christian ideals. For this reason, many young people engaged in sexual activity long before settling down with a partner.

A NOTE ON THE RISK OF GENERALIZATION

It is important to note that discussing "Indigenous Peoples of North America" is a broad generalization. With individual groups that numbered in the thousands before the arrival of colonizers, it would be as foolish to generalize them all as it would be to assume that the culture in Helsinki is the same as that in Lisbon because both cultures are indigenous European. So, while there were countless individual customs and social norms for partnership in pre-Columbian North America, this section stands merely to highlight how different it was from the Western status quo of today.

While it may be shocking by today's standards, the monogamous nature of some Indigenous groups was highly flexible. This included both men and women having the ability to terminate a marriage whenever they desired, as well as the practice of polygamy and fraternal polyandry (marrying two siblings). In some groups, like the Comanche, levirate marriage was practiced, where, should a man die, his brother would be next in line to marry his widow. Marriage ceremonies were slim to none. Instead, the bond was denoted by two (or more) individuals choosing to live together. Similarly, divorces were set up to be smooth as well, with no legal contracts required and both individuals retaining ownership of their personal belongings throughout the partnership. While this may all seem alien to us today, it is worth thinking how beneficial these systems would be to a smaller, more close-knit community. Where children from a marriage are not seen as "property" but the responsibility of the community as a whole, and where individuals are respected enough that no system is put in place to force them to stay in a situation they don't want to be in.

AIN'T NO CUPID

Given the frivolity of wedding ceremonies, it is no small wonder that the traditions and customs that develop around them are frequently over the top. This is to be expected when a tradition is refined over hundreds if not thousands of years *solely* on being the most exciting day of most people's lives. One of these countless celebrations of love comes from the Yugur people, an ethnic group indigenous to China's Gansu Province. The Yugur people are notorious for their lavish and over-the-top ceremonies that last on average two days, but can be longer still for families with the wealth and prestige to do so. And with good reason, as their name literally means "wealth and stability" in Chinese.

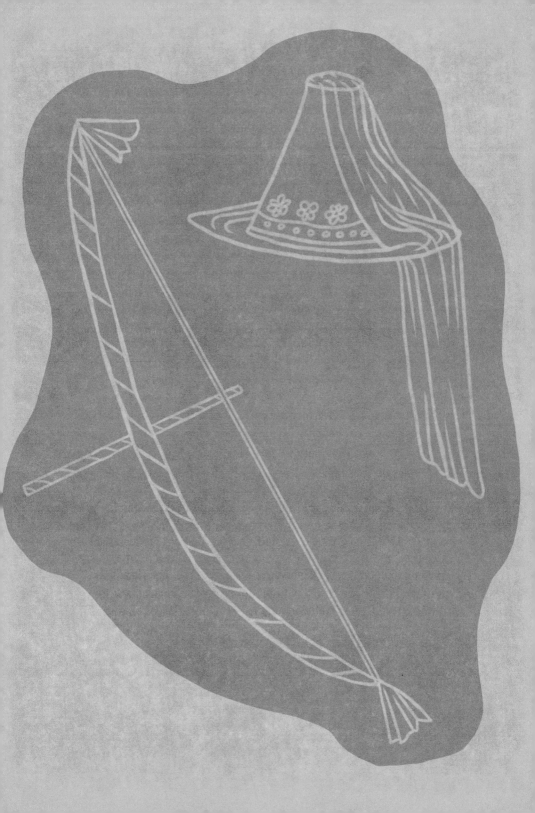

The outfits worn on this special day are worthy of a page in and of themselves, with the bride traditionally wearing a headdress made of silver and encrusted with sacred materials like coral, seashells, and jade. While not everyone goes for this now, the lavish presentation can still only be described as over the top. However, the most unique aspect of these already unique celebrations is that it is customary for the groom to shoot the bride with a bow and arrow. Not once, not twice, but three times.

Obviously, these arrows do not have points on them and the groom is certainly not shooting with hostile intent (I hope), so this element of the celebration causes no harm to the bejeweled bride. After the salvo, the groom collects the arrows and breaks all three of them in half. As the tradition dictates, this ceremony ensures the lasting bond between the two and a welcoming of the partnership with which they will carry on into their new lives. While the origins of this tradition are not precisely known, it is easy to infer the potential source. The Yugur are traditionally a nomadic people, and for thousands of years the ancestors of today's modern population would have been familiar with the art of bowmanship. Due to its significance within nomadic cultures, archery most likely found a way into the Yugurs' celebration of life and prosperity.

HIJRAS

Humankind does not all come out of one mold; we are creatures who are as diverse as any natural process, from how we look to how we love. The human capacity to express ourselves was, is, and always will be a fluid and highly personal experience. While today there are many policymakers and "leaders" who have seen it as their mission to define how others can love and express themselves, one must simply peer beyond the rhetoric to see that countless cultures have traditional and ancient acceptance for those who don't fit into the modern gender binary. One example of this is the hijras of India.

Hijras can be seen as a third gender within Hindu society; a group of people who identify neither with men nor with women, and instead find their own personal identities lying somewhere in between or outside them entirely. While in the modern world some may perceive this term as a definition synonymous with transgender, hijras are a broader community. While they do encompass transgender and intersex people, many hijras identify as being just that: a hijra. Neither a man, nor a woman, nor someone who is transitioning or looking to do so. This community, which has gone on to open its arms to many other gender-nonconforming groups, has a huge place of significance and respect within Hindu culture. It is in the *Ramayana*, one of the most important texts of the Hindu religion, that this group earned such a place of respect within the community.

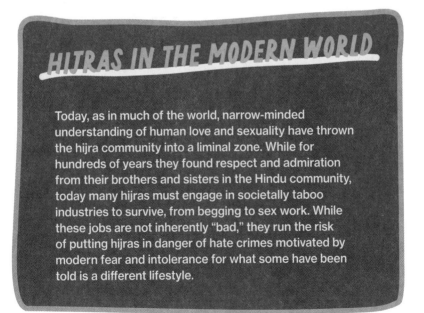

HIJRAS IN THE MODERN WORLD

Today, as in much of the world, narrow-minded understanding of human love and sexuality have thrown the hijra community into a liminal zone. While for hundreds of years they found respect and admiration from their brothers and sisters in the Hindu community, today many hijras must engage in societally taboo industries to survive, from begging to sex work. While these jobs are not inherently "bad," they run the risk of putting hijras in danger of hate crimes motivated by modern fear and intolerance for what some have been told is a different lifestyle.

The story goes that when Lord Rama was sent into exile, many of those who stood by him and supported his leadership followed him as he marched off into the forest. Lord Rama turned to them and instructed, "Men and women, please wipe your tears and go away." Heeding his command, the men and women dispersed. However, when Lord Rama returned from his exile fourteen years later, he found at the edge of the forest that some had never left and had sat waiting for him. They were neither men nor women, and so they sat and patiently waited for their lord's return. Moved by their devotion, Lord Rama blessed the hijras personally and instructed them to go on to bless others. It was from these divine origins that hijras became a sacred and integral part of Hinduism.

A WHALE OF A TALE

Today, tabua are still of huge cultural importance to the native Fijian population, which makes up more than 50 percent of the island's population. However, the outlawing of whale hunting has seen the supply of these teeth dwindle. This has led to recycling the tabua on the island and handing it from person to person. The only legitimate influx of new material comes from whales that wash up dead on the beaches, that may have their teeth scooped up before anything else can be done with the bodies. In this way, the Fijian population is able to keep this important tradition alive through their community without endangering wild populations of sperm whales.

TABUA

Courtship is a practice that predates us as a species. It can be found in just about every creature in the animal world that works to secure a mate through dances, gifts, or spectacular colors. Being animals, humans are no different. A particularly unique courtship custom comes from the small volcanic island chain of Fiji.

Within the native Fijian population whose culture has been defined by their oceanic surroundings, it is no small wonder that whale teeth have

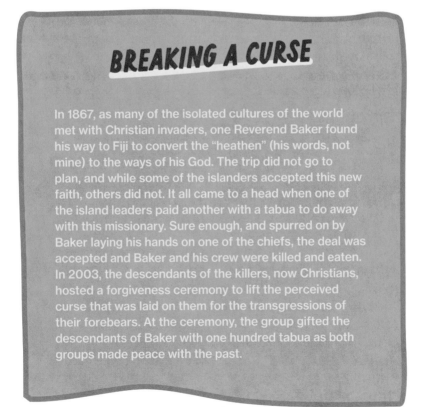

BREAKING A CURSE

In 1867, as many of the isolated cultures of the world met with Christian invaders, one Reverend Baker found his way to Fiji to convert the "heathen" (his words, not mine) to the ways of his God. The trip did not go to plan, and while some of the islanders accepted this new faith, others did not. It all came to a head when one of the island leaders paid another with a tabua to do away with this missionary. Sure enough, and spurred on by Baker laying his hands on one of the chiefs, the deal was accepted and Baker and his crew were killed and eaten. In 2003, the descendants of the killers, now Christians, hosted a forgiveness ceremony to lift the perceived curse that was laid on them for the transgressions of their forebears. At the ceremony, the group gifted the descendants of Baker with one hundred tabua as both groups made peace with the past.

found a place of importance amongst their traditions. Sperm whale teeth, which are referred to as *tabua*, or "sacred" in the native language, have been used for hundreds of years as part of the islanders' courtship processes.

The possession of these polished teeth would be tied closely to status. As valuable items, the more teeth you have, the higher your prestige. For marriage ceremonies, these teeth would be gifted to the bride by the groom, who may choose to wear the piece on a leather lanyard. Styles can range from polished to carved to even sharpened into long, tusk-like spikes. Courtship is not the only application of these highly valued teeth; they are also used for other ceremonies and events and traditionally have been passed as peace offerings between the island's different groups, used to settle debts, and even as payment for taking a life.

WHAT'S IN A NAME?

While we frequently associate the term "love" as one used toward a romantic partner, there are many kinds of love. One of these is the love toward your community. Your family, close friends, and those who helped shape you to be the person you are today. In many cultures around the world this close-knit cultural and communal love is one that quite literally ensured their survival, and from this love has sprung tradition. In the case of the Inuit people of the northern regions of North America, this tradition comes in the form of their names.

THE ENCYCLOPEDIA OF THE WEIRD AND WONDERFUL

In Inuit tradition, family ties are a crucial part of the social structure. Highlighting this is the tradition of giving children a namesake. When a child is born, it is tradition to find the name of someone else in the community to pass on to them. Sometimes it can be an elder or a family friend, while at other times it can be a deceased relative or someone else who no longer shares this mortal realm. This tradition holds huge significance in Inuit tradition, as it is seen to instill values, skills, or luck carried by the name into its new bearer. An interesting aspect of this is that these names can transcend the bearer's sex, meaning that it is not uncommon to give the name of a man to a baby girl, and vice versa. To the best of my understanding and research,

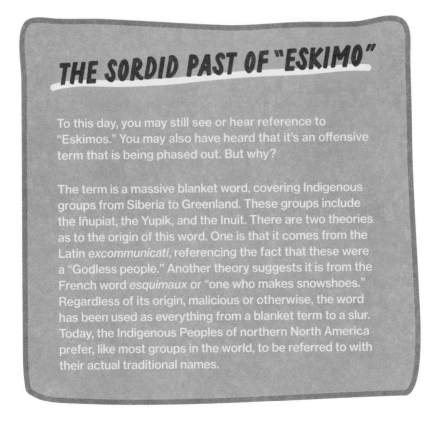

THE SORDID PAST OF "ESKIMO"

To this day, you may still see or hear reference to "Eskimos." You may also have heard that it's an offensive term that is being phased out. But why?

The term is a massive blanket word, covering Indigenous groups from Siberia to Greenland. These groups include the Iñupiat, the Yupik, and the Inuit. There are two theories as to the origin of this word. One is that it comes from the Latin excommunicati, referencing the fact that these were a "Godless people." Another theory suggests it is from the French word esquimaux or "one who makes snowshoes." Regardless of its origin, malicious or otherwise, the word has been used as everything from a blanket term to a slur. Today, the Indigenous Peoples of northern North America prefer, like most groups in the world, to be referred to with their actual traditional names.

this would imply that the idea of having gendered names is simply neither here nor there when considering this tradition. It is worth noting that using gender-neutral naming schemes is nothing new for much of the world. However, in places that currently exist under heavy Western influence, it has historically been par for the course to assign a child's name based on their sex.

This namesake tradition has recently been met with the great equalizer of many cultural practices: the colonization of North America and the attempted systematic annihilation of Indigenous cultures. Many of us may have heard of the residential schools which have recently fallen into the news spotlight as places where the bones of Indigenous children have been unearthed by the hundreds. Residential schools and similar institutions aimed to strip Indigenous children of their heritage, giving them new Christian names. In the case of the Inuit, they were given E-numbers: an identification number that replaced their traditional name.

While this barbaric assault on Indigenous culture has been abandoned, the effect it has had on the community is vast. Many Inuit people today are trying to return to this traditional practice despite hundreds of years of attempts to destroy it entirely.

SAW THAT COMING

Many wedding traditions around the world are developed in direct response to the environments in which the cultures that invented them exist. For this reason it is no small wonder that the people of Germany, a country that has historically been covered in dense, nigh-impregnable forests, has a tradition that is so wonderfully European that it just has to be included in this book. That is, of course, sawing a log in half.

Traditionally, this arboreal celebration happens directly after the wedding ceremony is complete and the newlyweds are officially bound in holy matrimony. The couple emerges outside and are presented with a log propped between two sawhorses. The two are then handed a two-person saw and set to work cutting the log in half. If you haven't used a two-person saw in your life, I couldn't recommend it more. It is an excellent example of something looking way easier than it is. Effectively using this serrated piece of metal requires complete cooperation and harmony between the pushing and pulling motions of both parties. The more in sync, the faster the job is done. And hell, even with some trial and error, the log is eventually cut in half to the boisterous celebration of the friends and family.

The ceremony itself is one that has a fairly intuitive symbolic meaning: it is the first challenge the two have to overcome as an official team. One where both need to carry their weight, cooperate with one another, and persist until the job is done. After completing this first task, the couple are able to proceed into life with sawdust on their clothes, a good story, and a potentially skewed perception of the challenges of marriage.

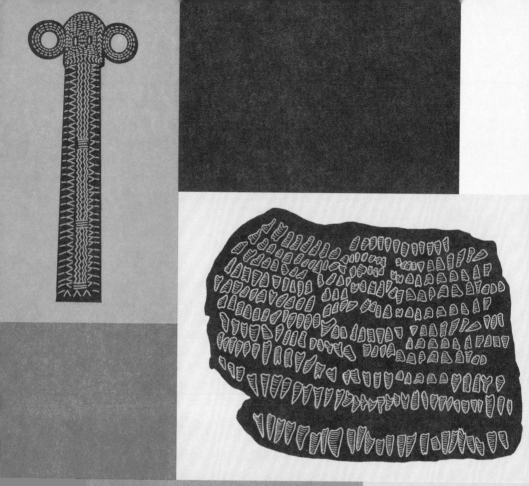
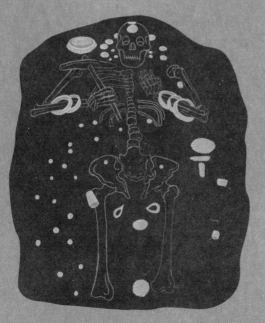

CHAPTER 7

FASHION AND BEAUTY

✦ ✦ ✦

It is no secret that humans take plenty of pride in their appearance. Like many animals, we portray our value as an individual to other members of our species through our outward image. With humans, who lack colorful plumage or an impressive set of antlers, much of our visual communication comes with how we choose to adorn ourselves. It is for this reason that fashion and beauty have come to be one of the most unique and varied forms of human expression throughout our existence.

FROM THE HEAVENS ABOVE

Today, fashion is a highly diverse part of human life and one that is constantly changing. It may be something that just seems to have always existed—and in a way you would be correct! While it is hard to pinpoint the "start of fashion," there is one discovery that seems to be the oldest evidence in the archaeological record, and it was created not by us, but by the Neanderthals.

Between 1899 and 1905, geologist Dragutin Gorjanović-Kramberger was conducting an excavation in a cave located near the Croatian town of Krapina. The remains found in the cave consisted of countless animal bones, many of which bore distinctive cut marks left behind by human processing. Among these assemblages were eight talons from the enormous white-tailed eagle, which, with a wingspan of up to 6 feet (1.8 m), is one of the largest birds of prey in the entirety of Europe. The eight talons that were found appear to have been intentionally manipulated, being severed from the bird's foot and burnished to give them a smooth, lustrous appearance. They also bear notches at their bases, indicating that these talons were not only altered to look better, but were actually worn as a form of jewelry.

What is so incredible about this find is that the talons were found in a bed that dates back a shocking 130,000 years, which I think is the oldest thing we have covered in this book so far. The likelihood that these decorations were carved by the hands of Neanderthals rather than our species continues to add credence to the idea that these were not brutish "cavemen." Instead, the care taken in this expression hints not only at artistic interpretation, but also the potential for spiritualism and some form of religion. Many have noted the Herculean effort it would be to catch one of these birds, and with their enormous silhouettes decorating the skies of this ancient world, it is no wonder that Neanderthals looked up to them and worked to incorporate their power into the decoration of themselves.

SPIN ME A YARN

Many of the clothes we wear in the modern world have one thing in common: they are created out of a woven fabric. From cotton to wool, to even acrylic fibers, the technology of converting fiber clusters into long strands which can in turn be made into large pieces of fabric has revolutionized the way we dress, warm, and protect ourselves. While weaving fibers is common in today's world, its origins date back a shocking 34,000 years.

In 2009, an archaeological dig in the country of Georgia yielded the remains of an ancient woven fiber. Archaeologists were able to identify these as coming from flax, a plant whose fibers are still used in making cloth to this day. However, rather than a fully woven piece of clothing being discovered, it came in a microscopic package.

While analyzing the soil for ancient pollen samples, paleobotanists discovered several small pieces of tiny fiber left behind by garments that had disintegrated over the last tens of thousands of years. Some of these flax fibers showed evidence of twisting, a critical step in creating thread or yarn. Others still showed even more signs of refinement, with evidence that they were dyed at one time. While it is unclear exactly what these threads were once a part of, the people who made them were likely better off for it.

While thread may seem like a fairly simple invention, it is one that would have increased humans' survivability by leaps and bounds.

Thread would allow for sewing, meaning that one could stitch together things such as hides into coats and, more importantly, shoes. This would have made a huge difference for humans who needed to survive in cold or alpine environments. The presence of dyed thread could also suggest that, beyond making thread, this group was making more refined articles of clothing that bore a much stronger cultural significance to a people who have been lost to time.

FASHION WITH A BITE

As long as we have had stuff we have needed a way to carry it. For our little accessories like coins, gum wrappers, and gift cards you will never use, there is no invention greater than the purse. Long before the wildly overpriced handbags of today, the ancient people of what is now Germany pioneered their own style for these convenient totes.

In an excavation of around three hundred Bronze Age graves near Leipzig, Germany, archaeologists stumbled upon an unusual grave good. Included in one of the burials and located along a flat horizon were over one hundred dogs' teeth. While dog remains are not an uncommon inclusion in Bronze Age graves throughout Europe, this one was particularly unusual due to its high quantity of teeth, which were all placed facing in the same direction. Through thorough analysis, archaeologists were able to infer that these teeth had once been affixed to a flap of a handbag or purse. Since it was made of leather, the bag did not withstand the test of time, leaving only the teeth behind.

Incredibly, this discovery dates back nearly 4,500 years, making it not only the oldest, but potentially the most confusing handbag ever found. The significance of this discovery is still not fully understood, with no evidence to suggest what this purse may have held or why it was necessary to decorate it with several dogs' worth of teeth. Some have put forward theories that it had a sort of ritual significance or, more simply, that it was a trendy fashion statement at the time. What is well known is that dogs were a common part of Bronze Age life and in some places were just as much companions as they were livestock. While we may never know the full story of the owner of this unusual bag, we can rest assured knowing that their fashion sense was way harder than any of ours.

I LOVE GOLD

When we think of fashion, gold reigns supreme. Humans' fascination with this shiny metal has led to wars, massacres, and the complete annihilation of entire civilizations. Despite the history of gold being soaked in blood, it remains one of the most fashionable materials that we can get our greedy little paws on. And like in all aspects, we don't change much, and our obsession with gold goes way, way back. Along the Black Sea coast in what is today the country of Bulgaria,

archaeologists happened upon the remains of a necropolis attributed to the Varna culture. This enormous burial zone contained a staggering total of 294 tombs dating to between 6,000 and 6,500 years ago. Collectively, these tombs yielded more than 3,000 golden artifacts that had been laid to rest with the dead. But one of these tombs stood out from the rest, boasting a particularly immense collection of golden artifacts.

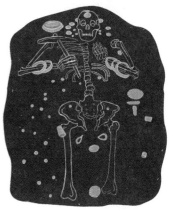

The grave site is unceremoniously referred to as "tomb 43" and contains the skeletal remains of a man who had likely once been of high importance. He was taller than most and was buried with enough gold to crash a regional economy. To put it into perspective, this man, whom other archaeologists refer to as Varna Man, but I will refer to as Papa Bling because I like fun, was buried with more gold than has been found from his time period. In the entire world. Ever.

Papa Bling was laid to rest with a golden scepter, a status symbol that persisted as recently as the European monarchies and is still a valuable ceremonial item. Along with this, he was also wearing five golden bracelets, two golden necklaces, and was surrounded by enough golden coins to make Scrooge McDuck have an aneurysm. But perhaps the icing on the cake is that this fabulously fashionable specimen of a man was buried with a solid gold penis sheath. While I may not have a lot of requests for my body post-mortem, I promise you that this is one idea I will be stealing. Then, someday when an archaeologist digs me up six thousand years from now, even they will be able to know that in life, I balled hard. So, whoever you are, you burly, gilded man, rest in bling.

TYRIAN PURPLE

The rich hue of purple has long been associated with royalty. It has been draped over the shoulders of monarchs, used in the tapestries that adorned the palaces and castles of the elite, and worn by great emperors and warlords who aimed to flex their prestigious muscles. But the story of purple is one that starts in a place that is anything but royal: a snail's ass.

The success of the purple dye in Tyre (in modern-day Lebanon) is due to the humble spiny murex sea snail, from which the dye is made. In each one of these snails was a tiny mucus gland conveniently located next to its anus. When dried, these royal snail anus glands would each yield an infinitesimal amount of dye. The production of a single tablespoon of this dye would require nearly a quarter of a million snails!

The conversion of snail ass to royal dye is one of the single greatest acts of alchemy humans have ever achieved. To make this bizarre transition, the snails were crushed and left in salt for the latter part of a week. After being sufficiently salted, the crushed salty catastrophe was boiled for upward of a week to extract the purple dye. But this dye wasn't enough to work on its own, so to add an extra binding agent the snails would be boiled in a mixture of wood ash and human urine. It is said that the stench of these vats of boiling urine and rotting shellfish was so rank that all operations had to take place outside the city walls because it would have been unbearable to do any of this near human dwellings.

The colors produced varied greatly from dark purples to magentas, and even to some rose reds and pinks. Despite this, the status symbol

PURPLE WONDERLAND

When we think of the royal purple color, many of us are thinking of Tyrian purple. The rich purple dye draws its name from Tyre, a Phoenician city that became one of the first major producers of the product as far back as the Bronze Age. Phoenicians were so well known for manufacturing Tyrian purple that the name Phoenicia translates roughly to "purple land."

of Tyrian purple spread like wildfire and from the Roman Empire to the English monarchy, purple reigned supreme. Even today it is not hard to see how much clout you would carry if you could afford to adorn yourself with the extracted dye of a million snail asses.

THE KUOSI SOCIETY

Fashion has always been used as a catalyst with which to convey status. When one thinks of just about any profession, there is a set of clothes or styles that come with it. This is nothing new, as for our entire existence we have used fashion to display our place within the ranks of society. The Bamileke region of Cameroon is home to one of the most spectacular examples of a piece of ritual fashion: the Kuosi Society elephant mask.

While the entire outfit worn by the Kuosi Society is spectacular in its whole, the mask itself is of particular interest. Typically fashioned on a base of raffia cloth, the mask is adorned with countless glass beads, protruding circular ears, and a long swinging "trunk." These masks incorporate myriad vibrant colors, such as reds, whites, yellows, and blues, set against a dark base cloth. To comfortably support the weight of these geometrically aligned beads, the mask itself is in the form of a hood, fully covering the wearer's head. These masks are fashioned to appear with the striking features of an elephant, exaggerating its ears and trunk. As spectacular as the masks are, the rest of the outfit completes the story, with a black cloak made of leopard hide and a headdress sporting a massive plume of red feathers.

Far from being a practical piece of fashion, these masks were used only a handful of times a year for certain ceremonies. Most commonly, these were performances for the *fon*, or king. The dancers who adorned themselves with this outfit aimed to display the power and prestige associated with animals such as the elephant and the leopard, whose power and strength were frequently symbolized in such political celebrations. In doing research for this book, I came across plenty of examples of these masks in American museums. While they are still beautiful, it is disheartening as an anthropologist to see them so removed from their context, where an outfit like this would have been brought to life through the dancing of the wearer, causing the static trunk and ears to sway with the movements.

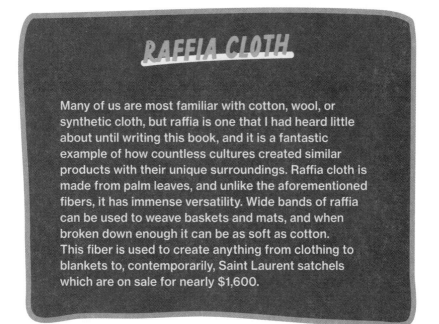

RAFFIA CLOTH

Many of us are most familiar with cotton, wool, or synthetic cloth, but raffia is one that I had heard little about until writing this book, and it is a fantastic example of how countless cultures created similar products with their unique surroundings. Raffia cloth is made from palm leaves, and unlike the aforementioned fibers, it has immense versatility. Wide bands of raffia can be used to weave baskets and mats, and when broken down enough it can be as soft as cotton. This fiber is used to create anything from clothing to blankets to, contemporarily, Saint Laurent satchels which are on sale for nearly $1,600.

TĀ MOKO

Given that this is a chapter on fashion and beauty, our minds may jump to a few forms of expression. My first thought would be clothing. Despite this being objectively the most common form of expressing one's fashion and beauty style today, considering that we all (for the most part) wear clothes, there are countless other ways that fashion, beauty, and tradition intersect. One of these is tattoo art, a practice with independent cultural instances all around the world, but perhaps the most striking of these is known as tā moko.

The Māori people of what is today known as New Zealand have practiced this form of art and storytelling since long before European colonization. While tattoos located on different parts of the body have different meanings, the tā moko, or face tattoos, are notable for their visibility and elaborate designs. Each tā moko is different; specific to the individual on which it is being done. Throughout a person's life, the tattoo can be altered and added to, growing with the life experience of the wearer. Traditionally, these tattoos were done using a sharp chisel dipped in ink. The chisel would be struck into the skin with a mallet, leaving behind a mark beneath the skin's surface. Alternatively, this process could also be done by scoring the skin and applying the ink afterward.

Beyond being a piece of personal storytelling, tā moko also incorporates lines for family history and heritage. This can be constants such as parents and grandparents as well as new additions such as children, a spouse, and even close friends. By slowly working on this piece, one's face becomes a documentation of their life's story, drawing on a set of traditional patterns that all bear their own meanings from health and prosperity to victory in battle.

THE ENCYCLOPEDIA OF THE WEIRD AND WONDERFUL

Despite the onslaught of European colonization, tā moko remains a crucial part of Māori life. Modern technology has allowed Māori artists to continue this tradition with a bit more precision and a lot less pain than a chisel, and so have effectively seen that this ancient tradition survives for the Māori people.

INDIAN YELLOW

The ability to change the color of fabrics and textiles has been an integral part of the human tradition of decorating ourselves. Like with Tyrian purple, there are some dyes that are obtained in ways that are less than savory. One of these is the chalky yellow dye known colloquially as Indian Yellow. This vibrant shade of gold has been used in India for both dying cloth and textiles and paint for decorating walls and canvases since the fifteenth century. It is a brilliant shade of golden orange and one that carries such a vibrance that it appears to get brighter when put in sunlight. The only caveat with this wonderful and diverse pigment is the methods through which it is produced.

The process of creating *piuri*, as the dye is traditionally known, begins with mango leaves. These thick calcium- and magnesium-salt-rich leaves are then fed to cattle that are put on an exclusive mango leaf diet. The urine from these cows is then collected and boiled to evaporate the liquid and leave behind the chalk-like yellow dust. After being clumped into balls by hand, the piuri is ready to be used as a paint or dye for anything that needs a hint of gold. The issue with this practice is the effect it has on the animals who help make it. By feeding a cow nothing but mango leaves and water, it is effectively being kept in a constant state of near starvation. Beyond this, mango leaves contain urushiol, an allergen found in plants like poison ivy.

The production of this dubious dye was banned in 1908 when cows earned their official holy status within the country. That being said, its vibrance in both paint and textile work was something that was highly coveted, leading to a campaign to recreate the color. By analyzing remaining examples of the dye, companies like Winsor & Newton have been able to recreate the color so it can still be used without the pesky ethical dilemma of animal abuse.

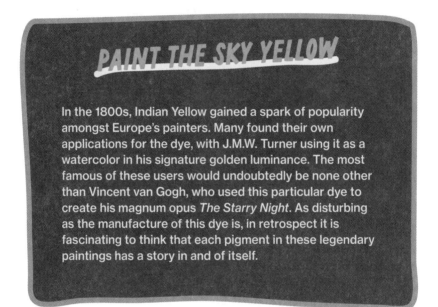

PAINT THE SKY YELLOW

In the 1800s, Indian Yellow gained a spark of popularity amongst Europe's painters. Many found their own applications for the dye, with J.M.W. Turner using it as a watercolor in his signature golden luminance. The most famous of these users would undoubtedly be none other than Vincent van Gogh, who used this particular dye to create his magnum opus *The Starry Night*. As disturbing as the manufacture of this dye is, in retrospect it is fascinating to think that each pigment in these legendary paintings has a story in and of itself.

POLKA DOTS

Patterned fabrics are as much a staple of our modern life as they have always been. With the capacity to mass-produce fabric, the options for patterns are virtually limitless. Of these countless patterns and styles, one that appears deceptively simple is the humble polka dot. Yet this pattern has more of a history than one may think.

The first recorded history of "polka dots" in a form similar to what we would see today comes from the 1700s. This was long before they were called polka dots, but we will get to that in a second. At this time, the pattern had two major challenges. First, it was hard to make; achieving perfect, evenly spaced circles without sophisticated weaving technology was very challenging. Second, and more importantly, this pattern was seen as taboo to wear. At this time in history many people associated spots with sickness and disease, likely reminding people of sores from diseases like smallpox and, in a bit of a more long-term cultural memory, the Black Death. Needless to say, polka dots were not "in."

By the 1800s the world took its first baby steps toward climate apocalypse with the Industrial Revolution. With this massive technological boom, factories were now able to produce more intricate patterned cloth, including our lovely polka dots. By this point

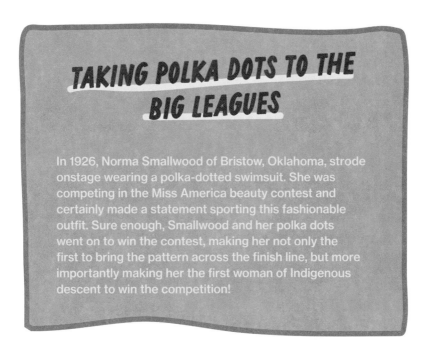

TAKING POLKA DOTS TO THE BIG LEAGUES

In 1926, Norma Smallwood of Bristow, Oklahoma, strode onstage wearing a polka-dotted swimsuit. She was competing in the Miss America beauty contest and certainly made a statement sporting this fashionable outfit. Sure enough, Smallwood and her polka dots went on to win the contest, making her not only the first to bring the pattern across the finish line, but more importantly making her the first woman of Indigenous descent to win the competition!

they had also shaken off their association with disease and began to form a new association: the polka!

In the early to mid-1800s, the traditional Czech dance known as the polka began to catch on in both Europe and the States. With this sudden fascination with the polka dance, a boom of products began to sprout up around it. Polka suspenders were sold along with the strangely named polka pudding. It is likely that during this time the circular pattern became associated with the dance, because by 1857 we get an early mention of the pattern by name from *Godey's Lady's Book*:

> "Scarf of muslin, for light summer wear, surrounded by a scalloped edge, embroidered in rows of round polka dots."

From here the polka dot went on to become an iconic part of twentieth-century culture, adorning the outfits of such icons as Marilyn Monroe and Minnie Mouse.

THE CRINOLINE

When considering the frequently extravagant fashion of the mid-to-late 1800s, many of our minds will wander to men with canes and top hats and women in large, bell-shaped dresses. These enormous domes were supported by a structure known as a crinoline: a piece of industrial-grade scaffolding used for the sole purpose of making a dress into a comically oversized satellite dish. The European-spawned tradition of excessively sized dresses began with a series of petticoats: multiple smaller layers that would build to create the perceived volume visible from the outside. Over time, whalebone hoops and even inflatable rings were implemented to achieve this magnitude, but by the mid-1850s a new design was created that thrust this fashion statement into the big leagues: the steel cage crinoline.

REVENGE OF THE CRINOLINE

As it so often does, history repeats itself. And the case of the crinoline dress is no different. Despite falling out of fashion before the end of the 1800s, by the 1950s this unusual fashion statement had a brief resurgence. In America's postwar-euphoria-driven desire to waste as much of everything as possible simply because they could, fabric found itself at the top of the list. And with no way to waste fabric quite like a crinoline, it was back in style! The crinolines of the 1950s were quite different from those one hundred years prior. They were much shorter and did not have the city block-encompassing effect of their forbears, but the swishy petticoats of these new shin-length designs were all the rage for people driving cars that weighed as much as a house.

By 1856, the steel crinoline was all the rage and found itself affixed to the waists of fancy ladies from the boulevards of Paris to the streets of Chicago. The design was simple: a wide cage made of long, thin pieces of steel that created a bell-like skeleton. The entire apparatus would have been affixed around the wearer's waist. This steel cage, patented by one W.S. Thompson, boomed in popularity. As demand spiked, supply increased to keep up. At peak demand, enough Sheffield steel was produced in a week to create more than half a million hoops.

As beautiful as they were, these crinoline dresses were not exactly practical. There were plenty of safety concerns that accompanied the liability of draping oneself in countless yards of loose fabric. Not only were the frills known to react poorly to open flames, but the loose ends tended not to mix well with the exposed wheels of carriages and wagons that now clogged the busy urban environments. There was also the obvious predicament of navigating oneself through literally any space while needing to maintain a several-foot perimeter on all sides. By the 1890s the legendary steel crinoline had fallen out of fashion and was, at least temporarily, retired to the annals of history.

FOREVER IN BLUE JEANS

Tim "Butch" McClain sat with his back to a cool stone wall. His breaths drew in crisp air that had wafted hundreds of feet down the mineshaft in which he sat. Many feet above him were the Cerro Gordo Mountains, a sun-scorched ridge slicing across the young state of California and providing a welcome variation in terrain from the nearby wasteland aptly dubbed Death Valley. His face was caked in grime and his hands looked as though they had been petrified. They were cracked, scarred, and bristling with calluses that all sat beneath a thick layer of rock dust and filth. Yet despite his rough appearance, his clothes were immaculate. He wore a fitted gray work shirt, reinforced in the elbows. His work boots shone in the lamplight and he sported a new edition to his wardrobe: a fashionable pair of riveted blue work pants from Levi Strauss & Co.

His beautifully pressed clothes and dashing appearance were all thanks to his better half, Maria. A fastidious woman, Maria took great pride in ensuring that every workday her "Butchy" left the house looking his best. "Cleanliness is next to godliness!" she had told him earlier that week after washing a day's worth of blasting aggregate off of his brand-new pants, "and you are His finest creation!" While he wouldn't admit it to his compatriots, Butch loved the amount of

fussing that Maria did over his wardrobe and he found himself carrying his head a little higher on days when his shirt had been freshly pressed.

As he sat next to the discarded pile of corn husks from his tamale lunch, legs not-so-subtly displaying their fashionable pants to all who passed, responsibility approached. His name was John. People called him Big John on account of him being big.

"Butch, I need ya help movin' da stuff outtada section uddah mine they're closin'," the big man barked.

On their feet, the two proceeded to undertake the Herculean effort of removing all the necessary equipment from the tunnel that was being shut down. Box after box of dynamite, pick heads, and nails were shuttled back up to storage by the throng of workers. After a rest-worthy number of trips, narrated entirely by Big John's gruff yet ceaseless storytelling, Butch prepared to take his last box up from the depths. As he heaved the case of copper fixtures from the ground and took a step forward, he caught an uneven stone. His ankle rolled and his weight shifted, and, with an exclamatory yell, he lurched forward, toward the miner in front of him. The two tumbled to the ground in a clatter of metal parts and curses. Both seemed unscathed as they were helped to their feet by their colleagues, but after a moment from the wreckage came a cry.

"My pants!"

It was Butch. He sat on the floor, hands outstretched as if he had committed a murder. His fabulously meticulous blue pants were pocked in rapidly drying candle wax from the arm load of newly extinguished candles held by the man into whom he tripped.

"It's nuthin, kid." Big John reached out to lift him up but Butch protested.

"Nothing? This is never gonna come out!"

"Work pants, Butch. The whole pointuh work pants isat you work innem. Wax ain't that bigofa . . . "

"My old lady breaks her back to make sure my clothes are clean!" the indignant miner continued. "I can't bring these back to her! She will *never* be able to get the wax out! It'll break her heart!"

He huffed and pulled a knee to his chest, picking at one of the small, opaque stains.

"Uhh . . . I gotta spare 'fya needem," piped up a stocky onlooker holding an armful of lanterns. Big John, who seemed not to fully understand the implied boundaries of personal belongings, had already picked up the clothes from the nearby table and tossed them to the disheveled man on the floor.

"Hey!" Butch said. "Hey, thanks man!" He hopped to his feet and in one fell swoop, whipped his pants down to his ankles, sending a small shockwave of surprise through the men around him. He stumbled out of the caked jeans before slipping on the new pair and proudly buttoned them. The rivets shone and they fit like a charm. He folded his old pair, now decorated in a constellation of waxy stars, and tossed them to the side of the shaft.

With the crisis averted, the men returned to work, and by that evening the last of the equipment had been removed. That section of mineshaft, and the pants within, was returned to its eternal subterranean darkness.

———————————————

There is no piece of modern fashion more iconic than blue jeans. They are simple yet elegant, casual yet sexy, and can be worn by anyone from a businessperson in a cubicle to a roofer wielding a nail gun and a large iced coffee. In fact, there is a good chance that you are wearing a pair of them as you read this and if you aren't, then luckily for you, I am. This iconic piece of fashion has its roots some 150 years ago to a humble tailor named Jacob Davis and a savvy businessman named Levi Strauss.

Strauss, whose first name has become synonymous with the iconic blue cotton pants, got his start peddling goods, including fabric, to the rapidly growing mining and logging communities that began to sprout up across the American West in the mid-1860s. His business model involved routing goods from wholesale suppliers in the cities to isolated mountain communities. Jacob Davis, one of Strauss's regulars, was a tailor based out of Reno, Nevada, who relied on cotton fabric to create his products. Davis had devised a unique way to create work pants out of Strauss's fabric.

By analyzing the frequent wear patterns on pants brought to him for repair, Davis was able to find the stress points on the garments. To improve these weak spots, he added metal rivets at places prone to tearing. These spots, such as in the corners of the pockets, held up much longer with this tiny fix. In fact, Davis was so pleased with his creation that he aimed to get it patented, but lacking the funds himself he asked his fabric supplier if he wanted to go in on the deal together.

On May 20, 1873, the two men, now business partners, had secured a patent for "improvement in fastening pocket-openings." From here, the first factory was opened to a smashing success. The first of these pants were known as "waist overalls" and would have been rather similar to the pants we wear today, though without the myriad fashion cuts. By the turn of the 1900s, Levi jeans were well on their way to being the bestselling men's work pants in the United States and officially achieved that record in the 1920s. It is truly spectacular how successful this single fashion invention has been. It has withstood the test of time, the ruthless culling of fashion statements, and continues to gracefully reign supreme as the most iconic and recognizable style of pants in the world.

FOREVER OUT OF BLUE JEANS

With an incredibly long history of production, it is no small wonder that finding an original pair of blue jeans is something that would send collectors directly into their bottomless wallets. In the deep belly of a mine shaft in Cerro Gordo, California, YouTuber Brent Underwood stumbled upon a pair of denim blue jeans left behind by miners over 130 years ago. When analyzed, the jeans were found to be in a shockingly excellent state of preservation. They had wax drips from miners' candles and even bore a tag on the back boldly claiming "The only kind made by white labor," a disturbing relic from the Chinese Exclusion Act of 1882. The jeans sold at auction for a staggering $87,000.

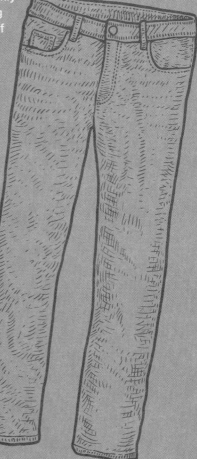

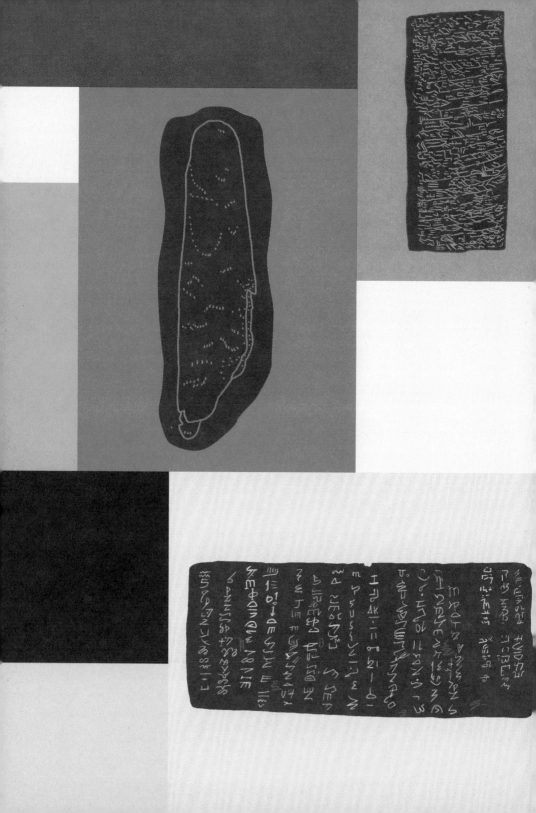

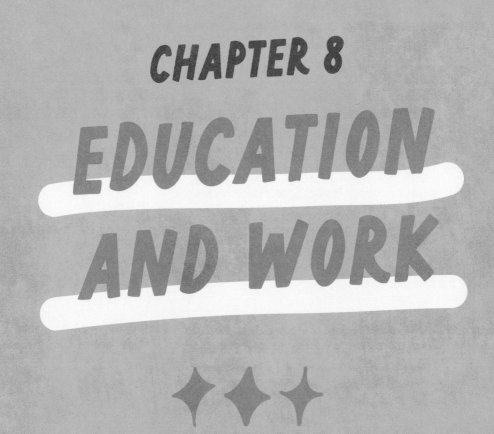

CHAPTER 8
EDUCATION
AND WORK

In the grand timeline of humanity's existence, our current perception of work and education is a recent development. While it is safe to say that the modern perspective is frequently negative (when was the last time you heard your partner tell you how great their commute to work was?), for the last several thousand years people like you and me have also slogged through their own versions of our modern 9-to-5 grind.

WE LOVE LEATHER

We do. We really, really love leather. Whether it's your work gloves, the seats in your car, or the jacket you wore to high school because you were sixteen and thought you were all that and a bag of chips, we can't get enough of this sturdy and diverse material. Leatherworking is an art and career that still very much exists today but got its start multiple thousands of years ago. In fact, the first to participate in this activity may not have even been *Homo sapiens*.

The discovery of small bone implements in southwest France changed the way we look at technological development. In a cave containing the forty-thousand-year-old remains of *Homo neanderthalensis* was found a thin bone implement that appeared to have been broken off a longer handle. After several of these tools were found, they were identified as burnishing implements known as a "lissoir." These tools are used to rub leather, giving it a shiny and water-resistant quality. Experimental archaeology with recreated artifacts confirmed that this was a highly likely use for this tool.

What is so incredible about this find is the fact that the exact same type of tool is still used now. A short, traditional bone implement that has been used by leather workers for over forty thousand years was potentially invented by a different species.

THE OLDEST JOB

When talking about the concept of work, one would be remiss not to mention the longest consistently running job position on the entire planet: agriculture. It may be low-hanging fruit (haha), but it cannot be stressed enough how this industry changed the world and allowed humans to become the Earth-dominating species we are today.

At the time of writing, the oldest evidence of farming has been pushed back from fifteen thousand to twenty-three thousand years old. Evidence from the Ohalo II site along the banks of Lake Galilee in modern Israel suggests that this ancient group was using rudimentary planting and harvesting equipment to take advantage of intentionally sown fields. Remains of ancient grains such as oats and barley have been found at the site in the remains of hand-operated stone-grinding stations that processed the cereals into flour.

As a job that stretches far into the obscuring shadows of prehistory, farming has seen many methods, developments, and overhauls. Humanity has ceaselessly found ways to make farming bigger and more reliable in an inconceivable number of ways throughout our history. Here are just a handful of agricultural practices that show the diversity of this crucial practice.

TERRACE FARMS

From pre-Columbian Mesoamerica to the rocky slopes of the Mediterranean, series of retaining walls have been built for thousands of years to create flat agricultural fields within the steep sides of hills and mountains. With the right maintenance, these walls reduce the erosion from rainfall that can spell disaster for mountainsides that are no longer held together by tree roots. This technology essentially made farming at any elevation possible, so long as there were rocks to build with and soil to back it up.

THE THREE SISTERS

The Paleo-Indigenous peoples of North America refined the practice of farming techniques that were not only sustainable for the consumers, but for the land itself. The Three Sisters is the name given to the botanical grouping of corn, beans, and squash. By growing these three together, each crop was able to enhance the growing capabilities of the others. The corn grew tall, allowing for the beans to have a climbing surface to spread their vines up. All the while squash grew on the ground and protected the roots of all the plants with its broad leaves. Furthermore, each plant in this system relied on a different amount of nutrients from the soil, meaning that the soil was never overtaxed by any one crop to the point that it lost its fertility. A major issue with modern agricultural practices today is the inverse of this practice. With large fields of one crop planted year after year in the same location, the soil is essentially drained of all its nutrients. This forces farmers to buy and spread artificial fertilizers to compensate for this imbalance.

IRRIGATION

Irrigation revolutionized agriculture. It allowed for areas that were previously devoid of plants, and at times life, to become hubs of food and economic production. While I could write an entirely separate book on irrigation, this section deserves a nod to the Indus Basin Irrigation System (or IBIS): the largest irrigation system in the world. While the concept of irrigation is ancient, this system is truly a new level of sophistication. The IBIS is a $300-*billion* system of nearly ninety dams and locks, seven hundred thousand tubed wells, and

forty-five canal command centers that operate twelve major river-linking canals. All of this combines to increase the productivity of forty-three thousand individual waterways throughout the country. As a result, its home country of Pakistan relies on this complex system for 25 percent of the region's gross domestic product (GDP) and 70 percent of all its financial exports. The land irrigated by this system is home to vast fields of wheat, cotton, oranges, and rice.

There are half a million examples of ways that humanity has harnessed the potential of agriculture. While the ones listed above are just three examples, they highlight the incredibly diverse methods we have found to feed our species. Today, 38 percent of the land on Earth is covered by agriculture. I will say that again, *38 percent*. A number so immense I can hardly fathom it. Our planet is ruled by this industry and those that work in it, carrying on an ancient tradition that has lasted for more than twenty thousand years.

REVENGE OF THE RED PEN

Through all the trials and tribulations of early education, there is one symbol that many students (assuming I am not the only one) have come to fear. That is, of course, the red pen. Acting as a symbol of criticism from authority, the red annotations can either be a mark of resounding success or of spectacular failure. This almost universal sign of critique and encouraged improvement is something that feels modern, but we are far from the first generation of students to be terrorized by the ominous red markings.

The discovery of a tablet dating back to Egypt's Middle Kingdom period (2000–1800 BCE) has shed light on the way ancient Egyptian students learned. The tablet, composed of a wooden board, would have layers of white gesso overlaid on top of various assignments in the same fashion that one would wipe a chalkboard. In the case of this tablet, it would appear that a scribe in training was practicing writing in hieratic.

Iny-su, the student who penned this ancient text, was apparently tasked with practicing writing in a formal style. Using a bit of creativity, the young man writes to his older brother Peh-ny-suh as if he were a wealthy man of great importance. While the content of his exercise may have been successful, his technical execution was apparently subpar for his instructor.

The document can be seen bearing multiple red marks. These are, as you won't be surprised, corrections and edits made by the teaching scribe. As disappointing as it must have been to have had his work critiqued, in true student fashion Iny-su likely broke out the gesso and a fresh board, and started from scratch.

THE ENCYCLOPEDIA OF THE WEIRD AND WONDERFUL

HIERATIC

When thinking of Egyptian writing systems, our minds will first go to the famous hieroglyphics. This writing structure has nearly one thousand characters, each of which has different sounds, meanings, and nuances when writing, reading, and interpreting them. For this reason, it wasn't exactly intuitive to use hieroglyphics to write quickly or exceptionally long texts unless you were a highly skilled scribe. So, a more simplified system of writing was developed and has been dubbed hieratic.

This writing system was comparable to a form of Egyptian cursive. Instead of focusing on the style and craftsmanship of each symbol and character, it served as a more functional form of writing. It was used for household and legal documents, invoices, and really any day-to-day activity that required the written word.

ANCIENT EGYPTIAN LATE-FOR-WORK NOTICES

For as long as there has been work, there have been days where workers have called out. Whether for legitimate reasons or merely an excuse to take a day off with the crew, humankind has tallied up a whole lot of sick days. And it is this very phenomenon that an Egyptian ostracon, now housed in the British Museum (because of course it is), has been able to share with the world of archaeology.

Dating to around 1250 BCE and discovered in the stonemason's village of Deir el-Medina alongside the Valley of the Kings, this tablet contains an itinerary of sick days taken from an ancient Egyptian workplace. The entire document is written in hieratic (see previous page) and contains around forty late-for-work notices and their reasons. Yet because of how different these reasons are from

OSTRACA

Is it a wizard's spell, a version of mancala made for orcas, or a new prescription drug to treat osteoporosis? I'm sure you will be shocked to know that it's far more exciting than any of those, because an ostracon is a chunk of limestone. These cheap, accessible, and easy-to-work pieces of rock were the sticky notes of the ancient world and found much of their use for household applications, from grocery lists to calling out from work because you got stung by a scorpion.

THE ENCYCLOPEDIA OF THE WEIRD AND WONDERFUL

those we have today, they offer a unique window into life in the New Kingdom era of Egypt.

Right off the bat these notifications consist of workers taking the day off after being stung by a scorpion as well as being busy "brewing beer." Admittedly I would also take the day off after being stung by a scorpion but, seeing as New England is not known for harboring many of these feisty arachnids, I doubt I'll have that to use as an excuse any time soon. And while brewing beer may not fly as an excuse with your boss today, at the time it was an important activity because beer was a primary part of the ancient Egyptian diet. This act was so important, in fact, that it was even associated with the Egyptian goddess of love and fertility, Hathor.

The most interesting of these notices references what would be translated into English as "wife/daughter bleeding." While this sounds like some sort of ancient 9-1-1 call, it is a reference to what is now more elegantly referred to as menstruation. It appears that in ancient

PERIOD LEAVE

At the time of writing (fall of 2022), Spain has become the first European country to approve paid menstrual leave. Which makes sense, since periods can decrease workplace productivity by 80 percent and is the number one reason that people who are twenty-five and under and have periods call out sick from school or work. Just remember, for all my fellow readers who don't have to experience periods firsthand, be like the ancient Egyptians and take the day off to be there for your partner or child.

Egypt it was commonplace for male workers to take time off to help their partners or children who were experiencing any of the many symptoms of their periods. However, it is great to see that after all this time and technological advancement, we have completely done away with this and now people who menstruate are made to work themselves into the ground just like the rest of us, no matter how much of their uterine lining they are shedding.

A BAD REVIEW

Whether it was a restaurant that served you food on dirty plates, a mechanic who charged you too much, or a mailed product that arrived only to be a cheap knock-off, we have all complained about something we've bought. Most of the time our frustrations are voiced to whoever finds themselves unfortunate enough to be near us at the time, but on occasion we will take it to the keyboard to leave a review. This may be a new way to express our discontent, but the core of it is as old as writing itself.

A clay tablet dating to the Old Babylonian period (circa 1750 BCE), and currently held in the British Museum, displays the dissatisfaction of an individual named Nanni. It would appear that Nanni had ordered a shipment of copper ore from Ea-Nasir that had to be shipped across the Persian Gulf. A shipment that was apparently so subpar that Nanni insisted on writing a complaint to this swindling merchant to give him a piece of his mind. The tablet, written in cuneiform, reads roughly as follows:

Nanni begins by informing the tablet's recipient, presumably a servant of Ea-Nasir, that he has a message for the merchant. He then proceeds to claim that Ea-Nasir promised him "fine-quality copper ingots" but apparently did not remain good on his word. Allegedly, and much to the frustrated writer's dismay, Nanni's servant who went to retrieve the ingots was told to either take 'em or leave 'em when they inquired about the metal's quality, a response which Nanni takes as a personal offense. Furthermore, Ea-Nasir is still in possession of the money used in this scam transaction, an issue that Nanni proposes to rectify by either having the money returned or new, high-quality metal sent instead. Should he receive such a poor-quality product again, Nanni threatens to show up himself and hand-pick the best-quality copper ingots from Ea-Nasir's stock to ensure he gets what he was promised.

While Nanni's complaint may have been penned (or stylus-ed?) nearly four thousand years ago, it reads in such a way that still resonates. And it seems like a fair reason to write a complaint. If someone had told *my* copper-fetcher something along the lines of "if you don't like it then leave" before sending me a full house of low-quality ingots, I would also be writing a furious request for a refund or at least a supply of quality copper ingots.

The tablet, found in the ruins of presumably the home of Ea-Nasir, is the only piece of this saga we know of today. However, I like to think that even if Nanni never got his desired copper, his angry review made the copper con artist lose at least a couple hours of sleep.

THE FIRST EXAM

There are few academic institutions more feared by students around the world than the exam. Exams, tests, quizzes, or any other form of retention assessment is make or break for many students and have subsequently earned their negative reputation among the student body. So, who do we have to thank for pioneering the process that would go on to become standardized testing from the SAT to the ACT to the GCSE?

This educational practice dates back more than two thousand years to ancient China's Qin Dynasty (220–205 BCE) and has origins that are quite admirable. As China grew in both strength and geographic scale it required complex and wide-reaching systems of government to control it. To fill these government slots, leaders would appoint family, friends, and business partners to positions of power—not unlike many of our favorite world governments today.

The ancient Chinese who saw the flaws in appointing these governing bodies through nepotism or favoritism aimed to find a new way to ensure that the bureaucrats in charge were qualified for the task. To do this, they established Keju, or Imperial Examinations, under Emperor Wudi's rule during the Han Dynasty (205 BCE–220 CE). Laying the groundwork for today's modern testing system, Keju worked to appoint people to positions of power based on skill and knowledge rather than connections and blood relations.

Scholars who applied to this process would find themselves tested in the Six Arts: archery, horseback riding, math, music, writing, and spiritual and cultural practices. Each of these fields worked to establish a benchmark of whether an applicant was ready to serve the people through a government based on Confucian values and principles, which was meant to be dedicated to the service and betterment of its people, guaranteeing their health and well-being.

FRATERNITY IN ANCIENT ATHENS

The concept of fraternities and sororities, sometimes referred to as "Greek life," is as ingrained in the modern American college experience as complaining about prerequisite classes and memorizing which way the wind has to blow in order to have a clandestine smoke out of a dorm window. Whether it's attending a formal function or getting absolutely trashed in a dark basement as speakers blast the worst music you have ever heard, the contemporary American college experience is truly one for the ages. But for this story we are going back to the very literal interpretation of Greek life.

A two-thousand-year-old tablet, held in the National Museum of Scotland, was found to be what is essentially an ancient Greek yearbook. The tablet, originally believed to be a plaster cast, bears the names of thirty-one young Athenians who had just graduated from their year of training at the Ephebate, where young Greek men, around the ages of eighteen to twenty years old, would be given their military training. The dedication at the end reading "of Caesar" is, confusingly to those of us who are not trained in classics, a reference to Roman Emperor Claudius who reigned from 41–54 CE, assigning an age range to the tablet. (By this point Greece was under the rule of the Roman Empire, explaining their allegiance to the emperor.) Despite all this time, the feelings of fraternity that developed among this group can still be seen on the ancient marble surface.

We know that the ancient inscriber of this tablet was named Attikos, and he was charged with recording the names of these thirty-one graduates. Likely part of a larger class of one hundred to two hundred students, some of the boys who made up this posse were Herakon, Athos, Dionysas, and Theogas. Interestingly, the last two are actually nicknames for "Dionysodoros" and "Theogenes," respectively. The recording of nicknames on a document of this importance is unusually informal for the time. But for anyone who has attended anything like a summer camp or even basic training, there will be no wonder that such a strong sense of friendship and camaraderie bloomed between this ancient squad.

OH HONEY, HONEY

Humanity's ability to apply our enormous and highly developed brains to achieve the things we desire in more efficient and accessible ways is what gave us the ability to do work. No other species on Earth can learn from and manipulate the world around them to achieve virtually any outcome desired. One of countless examples of this idea at work comes from one of our favorite sweet treats: honey.

We *love* honey, and for as long as we have occupied this planet, our ancestors have found ways to sneak, coax, coerce, or otherwise liberate the sticky treat from its fuzzy creators. Since this is no small feat, humanity had to invent a job dedicated to finding the most efficient and safest way to steal from insects. While today this process is beyond complex (as any apiarist will eagerly tell you) for much of human history it was ruled by one major technological advancement: the skep.

The skep is such a simple and effective piece of technology that it was used for nearly two thousand years and was only banned in the United States as of the 1990s. This ancient construction was essentially the prototype of a modern beehive, allowing humans to keep bees at their convenience rather than having to seek them out, thus allowing for the development of the apiarist profession.

The skep resembles an upside-down basket made of woven natural material and occasionally covered in mud or clay. The reason it resembles a basket is because that is quite literally what it started out as, with the shape and structure beginning as a half bushel grain measurement tool referred to in Old Norse as a *skeppa*. The use of skeps persisted for so long in Western Europe that those who worked in and around the hives developed the surname "Skepper," which still exists today!

When modified into a beehive, this structure did not change much. A single small opening was fashioned at the front to allow for bees to enter and exit the hive, which was hollow on the inside. This meant the bees had to build the entirety of the interior structure, a deviation from modern hives which typically have removable frames for both honey and brood. Which brings us to the major problem with the skep.

Despite this structure being one of the most common in the apiarist industry for thousands of years, they never really figured out how to get the bees out of it. Many skeps relied on the death of the colony to facilitate the removal of honey. This ranged from forcible removal of the comb and the hive's dispersal, killing the hive with sulfur smoke, or even crushing the entire structure to squeeze the honey out. Some skeps were eventually modified with removable lids, but the simple fact that the comb was adhered to the inside of the structure itself made it nearly impossible to not damage the hive during harvest.

While this process is not used nearly as commonly today, and those who do practice it do it with the full extent of technological advancement to make it far more sustainable, this was how humanity found the solution to our sweet tooth for much of its existence. The next time you see a honey bear on a store shelf or a white bee box in your community gardens, remember how long humanity's journey has been with this delightful little insect.

WE LOVE LATIN

For many students, the task of learning another language can be one that is mind-numbing at best. In many parts of the world the skill of being at *least* bilingual is seen as something that goes without saying, but in the United States it was certainly nothing short of pulling teeth for myself and many others. As long as we have had language, we have had to find ways to communicate with those who don't speak our native tongue. As the Roman Empire expanded it was this very problem that had to be solved.

While expanding past the borders of the regions that traditionally spoke Latin, methods needed to be developed to communicate with other regions and languages. One such method developed into a type of book known as the *colloquia*. These documents were almost like a modern language-to-language dictionary and helped Greek speakers learn how to hold conversations in Latin. Most of the original documents which were written between the second and fourth centuries CE had words and phrases in both Greek and Latin to allow for translation between the two.

Rather than focusing on structure and grammar, as we frequently learn in schools today, the colloquia were more akin to modern phrase books that put emphasis on real-world conversation structures. These lists included everything from simple question words like "where" to more complex phrases that would be used in conversation, from "please walk with me" to "let's go see him."

Today these documents have been compiled and refined, and can even still be purchased in various forms today. You can buy your own copy of the verbosely named *Colloquia of the Hermeneumata Pseudodositheana* online for the humble price of $110!

Interestingly, these ancient manuscripts have been used to inform modern lessons in the Latin language. By analyzing these documents, modern teachers and educators have found new methods of teaching material that focus more on conversational skills than grammar and sentence structure. If I ever had access to a time machine, I'd make a Roman take a Duolingo lesson.

AZTEC EDUCATION

The Aztec people, one of the most well-known pre-Columbian groups, had an education system that vastly surpassed other parts of the world in accessibility and scope. First and foremost, education was mandatory. Not only was this unusual for most parts of the world at the time, but the formal Aztec education system accommodated both young men and women, though the systems and lessons taught to both were different in many ways.

For boys around the age of fifteen there was the Telpochcalli. Translated into English as "house of youth," these education centers focused on training young men in standard military tactics and skills, much like the ancient Greek Ephebate (see page 177). As a civilization with a strong military, this schooling system was a vital part of maintaining the Aztec way of life. The Telpochcalli also taught other topics to these young men, such as law, religion, and history.

While women were not allowed in the Aztec military or government, they were obviously still an invaluable part of maintaining a balance in society. Around the age of thirteen, Aztec women began their own educational program, separate from the men. This program focused on the complexities of running a home and raising a family, including cooking, weaving, and sewing, as well as singing and dancing for rituals and ceremonies. Great care was taken to ensure that students were able to fully hone the complexities of the myriad tasks required to run a home and a family unit. This education system even prepared women for work outside the home, such as training to be what we today refer to as a midwife.

READING BETWEEN THE LINES

Whether it be homework, essays, or a worn-out third-hand textbook, every student has fallen into the trap of doodling. Each book tells a story in the margins through long-completed games of hangman and tic-tac-toe or, more simply, the infamous "tornado scribble." There is something about defacing your work that is more exciting than completing it. What may be less-common knowledge is that this habit has its own name. Referred to as marginalia, it dates back as long as humanity has touched pen to paper. Some of the most common and intriguing examples of this strange human tradition come from the margins of medieval European manuscripts.

These illustrations have myriad subjects: animals, people, plants, mythical beasts, and surreal interpretations of existing ones. The margins of these pages play host to a menagerie of medieval imagination. Some of these documents, held in the University of Glasgow, show a cross-eyed King Edward III complete with crown and royal cloak, several half-finished children's animal drawings— including a massive peacock being ridden by a tiny man—and my personal favorite: a disembodied penis in a basket pointing to an

A SNAIL OF A TALE

A bizarre yet recurring theme in medieval manuscript margins is snails. More specifically, knights fighting snails. The armored heroes can be seen on horseback, with helmets, lances, pikes, and all manner of angry steel facing off against naturally armored opponents of all sizes and colors. But why is this strange scene so common across so many manuscripts that seemingly have nothing to do with one another?

We have no idea! Many historians have aimed to find the meaning behind the recurring snail vs. knight meaning, yet there is no concrete explanation. Theories range from the snail being a proxy for a pesky and slimy foe to the scenes being an allegory for the inevitability of death. But my favorite of the theories is simply because the scene of a heavily armored soldier facing off against a garden pest is enough to get a chuckle out of anyone, medieval or modern-eval.

important part of the text. Certainly a cocky way to grab one's attention.

There are countless examples of these outlandish illustrations from countless sources penned by infinite authors, so I think the best way to demonstrate the sheer insanity of some of these drawings is to describe some of my favorites:

- ✦ An emaciated, bipedal dog playing a legless cat as a bagpipe.

- ✦ A knight, wearing only a helmet, riding a stick horse.

- ✦ Two nudists jousting on snails.

- ✦ A woman balancing a pitcher on her head while breastfeeding on worryingly tall stilts.

- ✦ Two naked headless men having a melee with a sword and a severed head.

- ✦ A man, wearing only a head wrap, simultaneously urinating and defecating into two different jars.

- ✦ A snail man with a snail-shell helmet impaling himself on his sword.

- ✦ And, finally, my personal favorite: two farmers harvesting the fruits of their penis tree.

THE VOYNICH MANUSCRIPT

When talking about the litany of strange and fantastic illustrations that adorn the pages of medieval manuscripts, it would be a shame not to mention what is likely the most bizarre and mysterious example of this phenomenon: the Voynich Manuscript. Far beyond a few strange illustrations doodled in the margins of otherwise deciphered texts, the Voynich Manuscript is a text in which its bizarre illustrations, and even unknown language, remain completely undeciphered.

As you may guess, the origins of this text are wholly unknown. Radiocarbon dating traces its creation to the late fifteenth century. The author also remains unknown. The book's contemporary title refers to a bookseller, Wilfrid Voynich, who acquired it in the early 1910s.

Nearly all of the book's 230 pages are illustrated and feature astronomical charts and recipes for pharmaceuticals and tinctures, as well as a truly unusual section displaying illustrations of nude women connected with tubes resembling some sort of medical process. The Manuscript has an overwhelming focus on botany, with 113 illustrations dedicated to plants alone. However, not a single one of these plants has ever been identified, leaving huge portions of the book as a field guide to otherwise completely unknown flora. To add to the tantalizing meaning behind the illustrations, each plant represented within the pages, from its tubers, to fruit, to leaves, is surrounded by careful annotations in the as of yet undeciphered language.

Interpretations of the text vary: an occult document, elaborate prank, or the hallucinogen-induced scrawlings of an unnamed fifteenth century European. Today, the Manuscript remains a mystery waiting to be solved by a mind capable of thinking outside the box. Considering that a full copy of the Manuscript is now available for purchase online, that mind could even be you.

INTO THE BELLY OF THE BEAST

The onset of the Industrial Revolution saw a massive shift in the way that work was conducted. Jobs that had previously been small-scale operations were able to be ramped up to a new, and at times horrifying, scale. Just one of the countless examples of jobs that arose to exploit a "disposable" workforce was the role of breaker boy.

Through the Allegheny and Appalachian Mountains of the eastern part of the United States runs one of the largest and most profitable veins of coal in the world. The "black gold" of these hills is the dense, black anthracite coal that burns hotter than Hell itself and powered the United States between the beginning of the nineteenth and the twentieth centuries.

As enormous operations were built to rip this highly lucrative mineral from the ground, new methods were needed to sort it from the worthless rocky rubble of its surroundings. Sure enough, this task fell into the hands of young children whose fathers worked breaking their backs in the mines. Too young to swing a pick, boys around the ages of eight to thirteen and as young as five were employed in the breakers, working for around forty to fifty cents a day (about $15 per day or around a dollar an hour in today's currency) to help support their desperate families.

The task of a breaker boy was simple: sit in a massive, dark, multi-story coal breaker from dawn till dusk and separate pieces of valuable coal from the worthless rubble. The conditions under which these children worked were nothing short of perilous. The air of the dingy breakers hung heavy with coal dust, which, when inhaled, led to the nightmarish malady known as black lung. The coal itself reacted with water, creating sulfuric acid (the same process that happens with carbon dioxide and water that creates acid rain) that would burn the ungloved hands of those handling it. Bosses who patrolled the

WHAT IS ANTHRACITE?

Despite what your most recent Minecraft playthrough may tell you, there is more than one type of coal. There is bituminous coal, subbituminous, lignite, and, of course, the black crown jewel: anthracite. This highly valuable rock is the rarest and most carbon-rich of the coal types and burns hotter, longer, and "cleaner" than the other variants. This is all thanks to its formation under higher degrees of heat and pressure, like in the case of the mountains of Pennsylvania, which experienced volcanic activity.

All coal started off the same. Massive, low-lying swampy forests of the Carboniferous Period were slowly covered and compressed, condensing millions of years of plant matter into the carbon-dense rocks. Therefore, many coal deposits have shale (a sedimentary rock) that contains fossils of ferns and strange, scaly trees. In fact, it is the rich coal deposits that we have today that give the carboniferous period its name!

breakers were even known to beat children found wearing gloves as it decreased their dexterity and therefore could impact efficiency and profits. But most unforgiving of all were the machines themselves. Sat in front of massive unstopping conveyer belts in a building designed to crush rock, breaker boys were known to lose fingers, limbs, and their lives to the hungry and unprotected machinery. Estimates range that in the 1880s there were upward of twenty thousand breaker boys working in the state of Pennsylvania alone.

Due to the uproar over the unsafe conditions that children were exposed to, a law was passed in 1885 that outlawed workers under the age of thirteen in coal breakers. While this was a step in the right direction, it did little to stop the flow of underage workers. Age checks were slim to none, and many families were still willing to allow their sons to work in the breakers as the exploitative practices of their employers saw Americans living in worse than poverty.

By the 1920s, the use of breaker boys had all but ended. While this is due to increased child labor protections at a federal level, it also had to do with the simple fact that the process had been mechanized, making breaker boys obsolete. To this day the story of the breaker boys is one that sits heavy with me. My family hails from those coal-rich hills and came to this country in search of work in these very mines. It is equal parts humbling and maddening to think of the generation of young men who were maimed, exploited, and killed all in the name of short-term profit. It is up to every working person today to ensure that the mistakes of the abuses of the past can never rear their heads again.

Ever since I was a kid, I have taken great joy in exploring abandoned places. Perhaps it's my desire to walk in the footsteps of the past or simply just a morbid fascination in seeing a place built by human hands returned to the gentle arms of Mother Earth. Whatever the case may be, at the age of eleven I found myself walking in the shadow of one of the largest abandoned structures I had ever seen.

On this humid summer day, my father and I were in the primordial hills of northeastern Pennsylvania where he had spent his own childhood years before, sneaking through the silent industrial ruins and peeling his dirt bike up piles of shattered earth. We made our way across a large plain of asphalt that was crisscrossed with cracks that seemed to be bleeding with green life. In front of us was a huge iron box whose face was pocked with broken windows. Seventy years ago, this monstrous building had been a coal breaker, one of many that littered the anthracite-rich fields near Scranton, Pennsylvania. But today, it was nothing more than a silent hulk.

The landscape around us was not the babbling brooks and whispering forests that one would expect from the Appalachians. Instead, we were ringed on all sides by piles of black refuse. Veritable mountains of debris that had been ripped from the earth where they had lain for 350 million years, only to be discarded at the surface to stain the streams and brooks black and orange. The only thing that could grow on these piles of filth are the ever-tolerant birch trees, whose thin white trunks poked out of the carnage. A small, but hopeful, sign of life.

As we approached the building, I remember feeling a profound sense of megalophobia. The sheer scale of this construction seemed to not only block light but absorb it entirely. It was as if the building itself oozed a sense of dread. Cool air wafted from inside the monolith and settled on the hot ground. It smelled like dust, mildew, and the bloodlike tang of iron rust.

We entered the ground floor of the building. It was silent save for the low whistle of wind through the shattered windows. The building was even bigger on the inside and metal pipes, chutes, and tubes wove up the walls and between the floors like the guts of a steel beast. I gazed in awe of this eerie environment for a long time, exploring the ground level of the refinery. I, of course, had a million questions that my father was quick to answer. Stories of mine collapses, strikes, and the ventilation pipe that he would throw rocks in as a kid and wait multiple seconds before hearing them strike the floor of the abandoned mineshafts that lay in eternal darkness far below.

But the story that stuck with me the most was those of the breaker boys. Children who would have been the same age I was at the time, working in some of the most horrific conditions one could imagine. While this breaker was newer and thus never housed breaker boys, I couldn't help but picture the faces of others my age who lived and died in the rooms like those around me.

My father pushed to have this site turned into a historic site. A place where the people of the modern world could walk the halls of this building to learn about the horrors of the past and be grateful for the gifts of the present. This building was an integral part of the community, not only because many families currently live in the valley, but because it's also a small chapter in the long story of American history.

In 2014, the Huber Breaker was demolished, wiped from the face of the Earth in a matter of years. Every memory, story, and tragedy that took place within its walls was laid low by the whim of some faceless businessman. Everything that ever happened in the Huber Breaker was crushed into scrap metal and sold for a grand total of $80,000. Today the site is empty. An abandoned lot with no development and no breaker. All that remains are the silent piles of debris, inhabited by ghosts and the thin, silent trunks of birch trees.

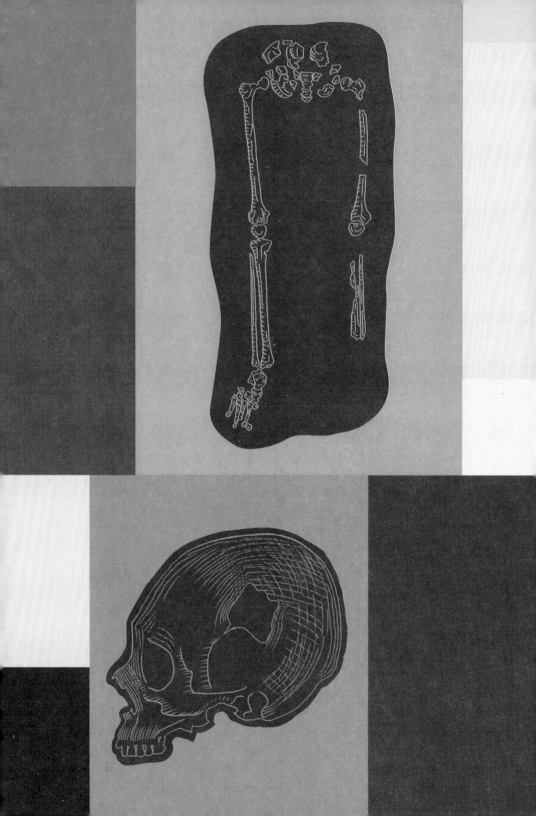

CHAPTER 9
SICKNESS AND HEALTH

✦ ✦ ✦

Despite billions of years of evolutionary refinement, humans are not perfect. Our bodies and minds are, for the most part, a resilient system and one that can bounce back when knocked down. But no matter how strong we are, we are not invulnerable. Whether it be a broken leg, a bad cold, or a debilitating birth defect, we have always been haunted through time by the fragility of our health. Yet one of the greatest displays of compassion around the world is the countless examples of care given by those who could provide to those who couldn't.

THE BORNEO AMPUTATION

A scream pierced the dense forest. From the jungle canopy a flock of hornbills exploded into flight, squawking their protest. Far below them, through the tangle of greenery that separated the sky from the forest floor, was another group of animals who, despite also walking on two legs, had no feathers. These animals were newcomers to the island, and they had made quite a splash. They were nearly unstoppable, boasting, in place of claws or fangs, sharpened stones, and adorning themselves in the skins, leaves, and plumage of all that stood in their way. They were highly social and, more importantly, highly intelligent. And one of them was injured.

On the jungle floor the group, numbering only around fifteen individuals, descended on the source of the noise. It was one of their children who now lay in the leaf litter and bleated their ear-piercing plea into the dense jungle. The first to get to the child was a tall man who stood a head above the rest. He knelt to inspect the damage. He let out a low exclamation as the extent of the injury became apparent. The child had fallen from the rocky outcrop next to them and must have caught their foot on the way down. As grim fate would have it, the angle was right to not just fracture, but splinter the base of their fragile shin bone. The damage was catastrophic, and the man sat back on his heels for a moment, mouth slack and eyes wide, speechless. The child screamed again and in an instant the man snapped back to reality and shot to his feet.

He barked a command at another man who was hurrying toward them. The running man stopped short and after nearly sliding on the leaf litter, he thrust his hand into his leather bag and dropped to a kneel. As he did this the tall one, still standing, addressed a matronly woman who was one of the few onlookers not in hysterics. She had done this before, and, without missing a beat, she began to pluck leaves from

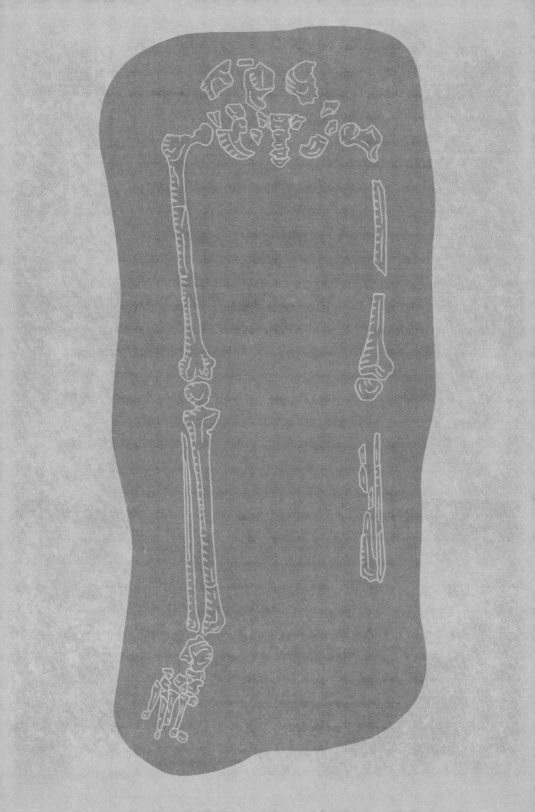

a nearby bush. The kneeling man produced a handful of sharpened stone blades from his bag. From choppers to blades so fine they were nearly transparent, the stones that lay strewn on the dirt before them were the work of nothing short of a master craftsman. The woman slapped the clump of leaves into the tall man's hand.

This was not the first time he had done this. In fact, it was not the first time any of them had done this. Just three full moons before, one of them in the group had contracted an infection in her hand and a similar attempt was made to save her life, but with no success. Despite this not being their first attempt at an amputation, this was the most spontaneous.

Like lightning, the leaves were mashed and placed in the mouth of the child whose consciousness was fading. The man with the bag of cutting blades sat, hands trembling, refining a selection of surgically sharp stones while the woman sang a haunting melody that sounded somewhere between a cry and a bird song. The tall man wiped the sweat from his brow into his mane of coarse black hair where it evaporated instantly. He knelt and, clutching the sharpest of the stones in his hand, took the child's leg into his lap. He took one last deep breath and drank in the forest air that hung silent except for the whisper of the wind and an unrecognizable bird call.

***

Many of today's medical procedures are ones that require myriad specialized medical equipment to conduct. This has led us to believe that it is only with this equipment that administering life-saving procedures is possible. However, a cave that was excavated in 2019 yielded the remains of an individual who had undergone a uniquely difficult procedure: an amputation.

The skeleton, whose sex has yet to be determined, was found buried in a sitting position within a cave located in the high mountains of the lush Indonesian island of Borneo. The individual is believed to have been in their early twenties when they died, and the cause of death is currently unknown. However, what *is* known is that this person had had their left leg cleanly severed in the middle of the shin. This is believed by archaeologists to be the first known example of an amputation.

As you may expect, an amputation is a messy task. One that contemporarily involves highly sterile environments and tools as well as a slurry of drugs that would put a Tool concert to shame. But this find is far, *far* older than the advent of bone saws and the release of *Ænema*. Through radiocarbon dating of the charcoal found in the same layer as the burial as well as electron spin resonance dating the individual's teeth, archaeologists were able to confirm that this individual lived nearly thirty thousand years ago.

The technical skill required to conduct an operation like this would have been immense. In the humid environments of Borneo's rainforest, infection can be a swift and painful killer, and yet the healing present on the bone indicates that this individual went on to live around eight years after the operation was complete. While this may seem surprising in a world where ancient people are viewed as little less than animals, it is not all that shocking when we remind ourselves that these people would have been *highly* in tune with their surroundings, having persisted there for thousands of years. It is more than likely that a knowledge of the countless pharmaceutical plants present in the jungle was a cornerstone in this patient's survival.

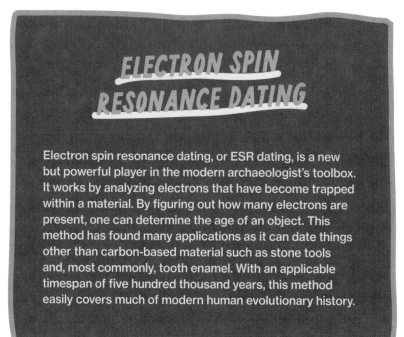

ELECTRON SPIN RESONANCE DATING

Electron spin resonance dating, or ESR dating, is a new but powerful player in the modern archaeologist's toolbox. It works by analyzing electrons that have become trapped within a material. By figuring out how many electrons are present, one can determine the age of an object. This method has found many applications as it can date things other than carbon-based material such as stone tools and, most commonly, tooth enamel. With an applicable timespan of five hundred thousand years, this method easily covers much of modern human evolutionary history.

THE POULNABRONE BABY

While some health complications arise later in life, there are others that are present at birth. One of these is a genetic discrepancy that results in an extra copy of chromosome 21, resulting in what we today call Down's Syndrome. While today there is a strong understanding of the causes and effects of this condition, it is far from new within the human world, or the animal kingdom as a whole. For our species, the oldest known example of Down's Syndrome comes from a burial on the rocky windswept coast of Ireland.

Beneath the stones of a megalithic site known as Poulnabrone in County Clare, Ireland, were found the remains of thirty-three

individuals. All but one was
younger than the age of thirty.
And the remains of one were
of a child who bore the
unmistakable signs
of Down's Syndrome.
Believed to be around
six months old when they died,
the infant was buried alongside several

other children beneath a monument that makes a modern headstone
look like a paperweight. The enormous standing stone monument,
known as a dolmen, has stood proudly above this burial for the
last 5,500 years. To our modern eye this find may seem surprising.
Perhaps we would have expected this child to have had a burial
that was vastly different from the others. Maybe something grander,
highlighting their difference from the rest, or on the flip side perhaps

THE POULNABRONE DOLMEN

The dolmen at the Poulnabrone site, creatively named the
Poulnabrone Dolmen, is a legendary archaeological site
in Ireland and a textbook example of a dolmen. In fact,
you have probably seen this dolmen quite literally in your
textbooks. While you may be familiar with what these
megalithic structures look like today, what you may not
know is that after their construction some were entirely
covered in dirt! This made them into a bit more of a cave
than a ring of standing stones, allowing ceremonies to
take place within them.

something grislier, like the rumors we discussed earlier of groups like the Spartans who left the young and "weak" to die.

Both of these would be interesting philosophies on which I'm sure you could write a paper, but remind yourself that this was not "a baby with Down's Syndrome," this was someone's child. Not someone who was loved because they were different, but because they were someone. While some archaeologists have expressed shock at the monumental grave under which they were found, this should be no surprise. While the modern world may tell us that we are defined by our "disabilities," it may be hard to see why this child wasn't treated differently. But to a family that was ripped apart 5,500 years ago, this infant was not a medical anomaly or a statistic, it was their child.

CABBAGE: THE GREATEST THING EVER

Medicinal plants are likely the oldest form of medicine ever used. Even some of our other animal cousins instinctively eat certain plants when feeling ill to get a sense of natural relief. While natural medicine is slowly making its way into the realm of western medicine, the people of the mighty Roman Empire found one plant that could apparently do everything: cabbage.

A staple in Europe for multiple thousands of years, the cabbage was a favorite of not only the Romans, but also the Greeks, Egyptians, and other cultures whom you read books about as a kid and sowed the seeds that made you buy this one (thank you!). But the Romans took their cabbage very seriously because to them it was not just a food, but a cure all. According to Cato the Elder, who penned a two-thousand-word-long thesis on how great cabbages are, the leafy plant could fix headaches, digestive problems, poor eyesight, and even could be topically applied on wounds to heal them. Chrysippus of Cnidus claimed that Athenian women would eat it after giving birth. Why? Not sure. But that's nothing compared to ancient Greek physician Erastistratus, who claimed that somehow cabbage could cure someone who was paralyzed.

But the claims continued to get more and more ridiculous, and like a snake oil salesman, it wasn't long before cabbage was touted as the cure for literally everything. The most extreme of these claims once again comes from Cato, who claimed that it had the ability to cure most, if not every disease. Cato goes on to explain that huffing boiled

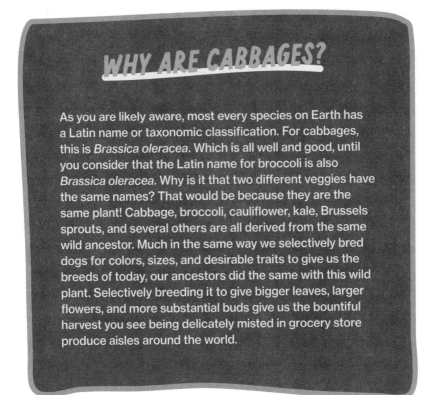

WHY ARE CABBAGES?

As you are likely aware, most every species on Earth has a Latin name or taxonomic classification. For cabbages, this is *Brassica oleracea*. Which is all well and good, until you consider that the Latin name for broccoli is also *Brassica oleracea*. Why is it that two different veggies have the same names? That would be because they are the same plant! Cabbage, broccoli, cauliflower, kale, Brussels sprouts, and several others are all derived from the same wild ancestor. Much in the same way we selectively bred dogs for colors, sizes, and desirable traits to give us the breeds of today, our ancestors did the same with this wild plant. Selectively breeding it to give bigger leaves, larger flowers, and more substantial buds give us the bountiful harvest you see being delicately misted in grocery store produce aisles around the world.

cabbage fumes could increase fertility and that a good old-fashioned bath in the urine of someone who had eaten a respectable amount of cabbages could set you straight from just about everything. While today we know cabbage can act as an anti-inflammatory and a blood pressure regulator, I don't think you would be able to find a single doctor today who would recommend a cabbage urine shower.

A REAL HEADACHE

In the realm of modern surgeries, there are few procedures that are as synonymous with technical difficulty and anatomic knowledge as brain surgery. And with good reason. The brain itself, being the powerhouse of the entire body, is a highly fragile and specialized organ that can sustain permanent damage when not handled correctly. But this process we see as a lifesaver in the modern world was pioneered more than four thousand years ago by the Indigenous inhabitants of the Americas.

The discovery of a skeleton in what is now known as the state of Alabama bears the oldest evidence of this complex procedure. The man's skull has an oval hole cut through the front of it with expert precision. Healing around the area suggests that the surgery went on to heal for over a year before the patient died. While his exact cause of death is unknown, the presence of healed fractures on his left arm, left leg, and collarbone suggest he may have suffered a serious injury that could have resulted in fluid pressure buildup in the skull that, if left untreated, could have been fatal. It is more than likely that this surgery greatly extended his life. But what is even more interesting than this one example is the evidence that this field of medicine developed greatly throughout time in the pre-Columbian world.

In South America, many skulls bearing different-sized holes in different parts of the skull have been found. The skulls of Peru have been studied extensively and yielded astonishing results. The oldest grouping of Peruvian skulls found dates to around 400–200 BCE, and the process seems to have had about a 40 percent survival rate. This is determined by whether or not the bone shows signs of healing after the procedure. From 1000 to 1400, more than half of the patients survived, and just before the Incan Empire was invaded by the Spanish, the procedure had a survival rate of 80 percent. There is even a cluster of skulls from the Peruvian highlands dating to around 1100 that indicate a survival rate of up to 90 percent! This research is shocking for many reasons. Perhaps the only part that isn't surprising is that these ancient people, like us, would do anything to save their injured friends and family even if it meant taking the risk of death.

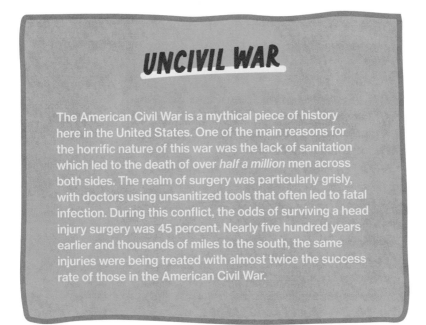

UNCIVIL WAR

The American Civil War is a mythical piece of history here in the United States. One of the main reasons for the horrific nature of this war was the lack of sanitation which led to the death of over *half a million* men across both sides. The realm of surgery was particularly grisly, with doctors using unsanitized tools that often led to fatal infection. During this conflict, the odds of surviving a head injury surgery was 45 percent. Nearly five hundred years earlier and thousands of miles to the south, the same injuries were being treated with almost twice the success rate of those in the American Civil War.

DEFEATING A GIANT

For much of the modern developed world it can be hard to see how many lives have been improved, and of course saved, by the successful elimination of diseases that ravaged much of humanity. One of humanity's greatest enemies of all time was none other than the highly contagious virus *Measles morbillivirus*, more commonly referred to by its shorthand: measles.

The first recorded evidence of measles dates to ninth-century Persia in the writings of the Islamic Golden Age physician and alchemist Abū Bakr Muhammad Zakariyyā al-Rāzī. The works of Rāzī were highly influential, being the first to outline the differences between smallpox and measles. In his book entitled *Kitab al-Jadari wa 'l-Hasba*, literally *The Book About Smallpox and Measles*, he discusses how to identify the early signs of the virus present in a contagious person who has not yet succumbed to a full outbreak.

In 1757, the understanding of measles and of viruses was drastically changed when Francis Home learned that the disease could be spread through blood. To test this, the Scottish doctor did what anyone would do and transferred the blood of a measles patient to the body of someone who didn't have, and had never had measles, and what do ya know! The guy got measles. Man, I love science.

As European colonization spread across the planet, groups that had had no previous exposure to the virus were decimated by it. Places like the Faroe Islands, Fiji, and Rotuma encountered massive epidemics that saw the death of thousands. Throughout the rest of the world the death count remained enormous. Before a solution was found, an estimated thirty million people were infected per year, with two million of those, many of whom were children, not surviving the virus's effects.

By 1963, a measles vaccine had been approved for use to shocking success. By the mid-1970s the vaccine had been drastically improved and efforts were being taken to eliminate the disease from the United States. Sure enough, by the year 2000, the measles virus had been functionally eliminated within the country. Globally, measles continues to kill around 150,000 people, many of whom are in countries with less vaccine access than the United States. While it was a slogan originally coined for the borders of the American states, with enough time the human species will undoubtedly succeed in "making measles a memory."

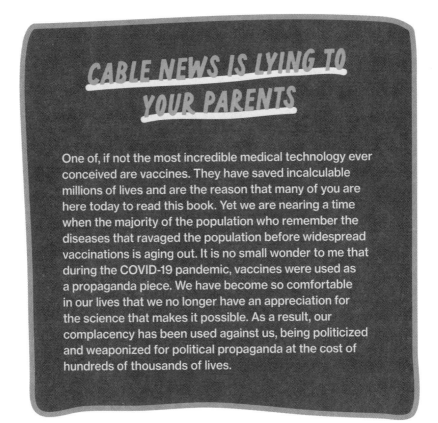

CABLE NEWS IS LYING TO YOUR PARENTS

One of, if not the most incredible medical technology ever conceived are vaccines. They have saved incalculable millions of lives and are the reason that many of you are here today to read this book. Yet we are nearing a time when the majority of the population who remember the diseases that ravaged the population before widespread vaccinations is aging out. It is no small wonder to me that during the COVID-19 pandemic, vaccines were used as a propaganda piece. We have become so comfortable in our lives that we no longer have an appreciation for the science that makes it possible. As a result, our complacency has been used against us, being politicized and weaponized for political propaganda at the cost of hundreds of thousands of lives.

THE RIDE OF A LIFETIME

The Black Death is the single most catastrophic pandemic ever to strike the human population in modern history. With an estimated death toll ranging from fifty to two hundred *million* people, Europe saw between 40 and 60 percent of its population wiped from the Earth in just a matter of years. The entire calamity was caused by a bacteria called *Yersinia pestis,* whose scar on humankind is so apparent that it is referred to in modern medicine simply as "the plague." While today we have a strong understanding of how this disease works, in the 1350s it was anyone's guess. But that didn't stop people from figuring out how it spread pretty quickly.

One of the most unusual occurrences of the early years of the plague is also attributed to its immense spread across much of Europe. In 1344, the Mongol army, commanded by Khan Djanibek, laid siege to the Crimean port city of Caffa. The siege, which started as revenge for a Mongol who was killed by an Italian, soon became a nightmare as the plague began to spread through the Mongol army's camp. Primary sources who witnessed the siege describe the dead outside the walls being piled like mountains. Within the walls, the Christian residents were thrilled, claiming that this was God's punishment for the transgressions of their enemies against Him. But this celebration was short-lived as Djanibek decided to send his own divine judgment to the inhabitants of the walled city.

Once in the catapults, the rotting, diseased corpses of hundreds of plague-ridden warriors were hurled over the city's walls. This wreaked absolute havoc within the city and soon, sure enough, the divine wrath of God had found them as well. Plague ripped through the city and the panicked inhabitants struggled to find their way out and away from the chaos. In doing this, four merchant ships escaped the city. They sailed to the cities of Sicily, Marseille, and Valencia, bringing with them their cargo of refugees and the invisible wrath of God that spread the blood-gorged fleas on rats infected with *Yersinia pestis* that flooded from the ship's hold.

PINS AND NEEDLES

One of the most misunderstood medical practices in the western world is acupuncture. Growing up I was quite put off by the practice as I couldn't wrap my head around how poking someone with needles had any benefit other than low-grade torture. While in the last several decades the practice has been finding more widespread acceptance and application within Western medicine, its history is far older than that of prescription painkillers and the for-profit healthcare system.

Since there is no written documentation for the first examples of acupuncture, the oldest clues hail from scant archaeological evidence. There is also a theory that the modern practice of acupuncture started with the application of warm rocks to various pressure points on the body. You have probably seen this strategy persisting to this day within the realm of massage therapy.

The first concrete evidence for acupuncture as we would recognize it today comes from a document called *The Yellow Emperor's Classic of Internal Medicine*, which was penned in 100 BCE. This tome is a collection of what are likely hundreds, if not thousands, of years of knowledge in the field of traditional Chinese medicine. The text describes acupuncture as helping with the life force that flowed through the body, which was known as Qi. This Qi was believed to run along certain meridians within the body and could be manipulated through acupuncture. Over the next several hundred years the process would be refined to give acupuncturists more specialized pressure points.

By the mid-1400s in the Ming Dynasty, *The Great Compendium of Acupuncture and Moxibustion* was written and discussed not only the process of moxibustion, or application of heat for therapeutic purposes, but also 365 points on the human body that an acupuncturist could use to channel a patient's Qi. This text went on to be the foundational text for modern acupuncture.

ICEUPUNCTURE

Thousands of miles away from China on the snowy peaks of the Ötztal Alps comes another example of what some believe to be a form of acupuncture. The body of Ötzi the Iceman, my favorite archaeological discovery of all time, bears more than seventy unique tattoo lines on his lower back and legs. While the purpose of these tattoos is not precisely known, the fact that they are located around joint areas such as knees and the lumbar region could suggest they had medicinal purposes. Supporting this is the fact that Ötzi is the oldest recorded human case of Lyme disease, and despite being in his forties when he died, was suffering from arthritis. Some archaeologists and physicians believe these tattoos to be another ancient form of therapeutic manipulation of skin and muscle.

AN UNHOLY WAR

For as long as humans have known what sickness is, it has been used as a weapon. While today the use of chemical and biological weapons is outlawed under the Geneva Conventions (not that that stops anyone), for much of our history the weaponization of the incurable was par for the course as armies worked to conquer land and people. One of the most well-known of these examples comes from the European conquest of North America: the infamous story of the smallpox blankets.

While European disease was intentionally spread among Indigenous populations essentially since contact, the first recorded instance of infected blankets didn't come until the 1700s. When referring to this ignoble part of early American history, the likely source of the story is from the siege of Fort Pitt, the site of which is the modern city of Pittsburgh, Pennsylvania. In 1763, at the start of Pontiac's Rebellion, a confederation of thirteen Great Lakes Indigenous groups laid siege to the British fort. As the story goes, on June 24, Captain Simeon Ecuyer attempted parlay by giving the Indigenous Peoples a handful of items including three blankets and a handkerchief.

Within the walls of Fort Pitt, an outbreak of smallpox had justified the construction of a containment ward. And it was from this hotbed of disease that these blankets were taken. While it is unclear whether or not Ecuyer acted on command or by his own volition, it apparently made no difference to his compatriots. Captain William Trent wrote of the incident: "We gave them two blankets and a handkerchief out of the smallpox hospital. I hope it will have the desired effect." On July 7, Sir Jeffery Amherst, the off-side commanding force of all at the fort, wrote to the British: "Could it not be contrived to send the smallpox among those disaffected tribes of Indians? We must, on this occasion, use every stratagem in our power to reduce them."

In response, on July 13 the fort's colonel responded that he would indeed "try to inoculate the bastards with some blankets that may fall into their hands." It is worth noting in this case that inoculation does not carry the definition of health that it does today.

It is likely that throughout the European conquest of North America there were countless examples of such barbarism. While many have been lost to the annals of history, it is impossible to say how many lives were lost to intentional spread of disease or simply turning the other cheek and allowing it to happen.

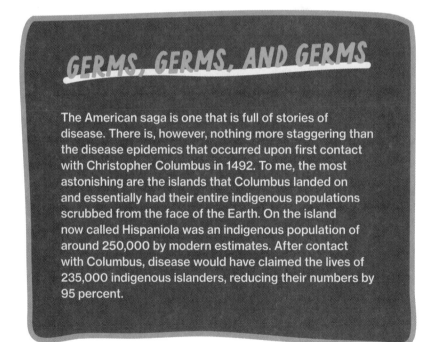

GERMS, GERMS, AND GERMS

The American saga is one that is full of stories of disease. There is, however, nothing more staggering than the disease epidemics that occurred upon first contact with Christopher Columbus in 1492. To me, the most astonishing are the islands that Columbus landed on and essentially had their entire indigenous populations scrubbed from the face of the Earth. On the island now called Hispaniola was an indigenous population of around 250,000 by modern estimates. After contact with Columbus, disease would have claimed the lives of 235,000 indigenous islanders, reducing their numbers by 95 percent.

THE ENCYCLOPEDIA OF THE WEIRD AND WONDERFUL

BLOWING YOUR NOSE

The myriad insane medicines prescribed to people throughout modern history is the topic of countless dinner table fun facts. From bloodletting with leeches to making children calm down with heroin, it seems that historically death could be seen as a successful cure. However, of all of these, my personal favorite is one that will be near and dear to the heart and sinuses of anyone who struggles with spring allergies: treating hay fever with cocaine.

In the late 1880s, physicians across the United States and Europe touted the curative powers of cocaine in addressing the debilitating effects of hay fever. In an 1885 paper in the *London Lancet* by Roberts Bartholow, MD, the author opens with this phenomenal line: "The remarkable success which has attended the use of Cocaine in cases of Hay Fever, is one of the most interesting developments in pharmaceutical history . . . " And to that, I'd have to agree. "Interesting" is certainly a word to use for it. Along with hilarious and absolutely insane. The article goes on to discuss how cocaine acts to decrease sensitivity of the mucus membranes through the application of special tablets.

The public apparently were very receptive to this paper, as one John Watson writes back to the *London Lancet*, telling his tale of woe about his hay fever and inquiring further as to whether this cure could help treat his case, which he notes is particularly debilitating in heat and sunlight. W. M. Abbots writes back, claiming that, "It is precisely in such cases as Mr. Watson graphically describes, from a personal experience, that Cocaine presents satisfactory results." While verbose, this sentence can be boiled down to simply a doctor saying, "Hay fever? Just do a line."

A Chicago journal writer, E. Fletcher Ingals, MD, responds in his own article where he remarks that while cocaine *is* effective at treating hay fever, it is worth noting that "continued use of the drug renders it necessary for the patient to take more and more of it for relief . . . " This is the 1885 equivalent of your high school friend explaining what a "tolerance break" is. It seems here the official deduction is that cocaine is good for hay fever, in moderation.

Please, obviously, for the love of God, do not actually try this.

SELLING SNAKE OIL

You are likely familiar with the phrase "snake oil salesman" or simply referring to something as "snake oil." Today, this term is synonymous with a grifter, someone who aims to make a quick buck off an unsuspecting group of people, while snake oil itself refers to a product or pitch that is simply a lie. The origins of this phrase are, as you'd expect, even more interesting than the phrase itself.

The term originates in the American West as rail lines were being sliced along the country's back. At this time a massive portion of the rail building labor force came from Chinese railroad workers. They were paid horrifyingly low wages, were forced into equally horrifying living conditions, and worked in dangerous environments to connect the American continent. It is estimated that between 1849 and 1882, 180,000 Chinese migrant workers came to the United States to work on the rail lines. And with the workers came their traditions and customs from back home.

Just one of these cultural tidbits that made its way across the ocean was the traditional medicine which was, quite literally, snake oil. Far from the phony product we would associate it with today, this snake oil came from the Chinese water snake. It produced an elixir that could treat arthritis due to it having a high concentration of omega-3 acids. Traditionally, workers would apply it as a topical solution to joints to relieve the stress of a day's work. American workers were so stunned by the efficacy of their Chinese compatriots that they set out to make their own.

With no Chinese water snakes on hand in the continental United States, wannabe physicians resorted to extracting the oil from rattlesnakes instead. This, of course, did not work. But the craze spread and by 1893 a man named Clark Stanley (who would refer to himself as the Rattlesnake King) unveiled his snake oil before a live audience at the Chicago World Expo. Claiming to have learned the practice from a Hopi medicine man, Stanley showed the preparation of the oil from a rattlesnake's liver. The craze caught on, and people bought the product en masse. In 1917, a federal investigation found that not only did rattlesnake oil contain only a third of the active ingredient of the water snake variant, but that Stanley's oil wasn't even snake oil. It was found that the bottles contained mineral oil and various plant extracts. And just like that, one fraudulent doctor turned an ancient medicine into a synonym for fraud and exploitation.

CHAPTER 10
MEMENTO MORI

✦ ✦ ✦

Each of us lives a unique life. While we may share common experiences, values, and beliefs with those around us, the way we spend our time on this Earth is entirely up to us. But no matter how we fill our days, life is a ticking clock, slowly counting down to one great inevitability: death. Humans are highly intelligent creatures, and as a result, death has always motivated, mystified, and terrified us. Throughout time, the dead have left the living searching for answers as we grapple with the unavoidable reality that, one day, we too will join them. But no matter the spiritual conclusions drawn in trying to unwrap the great unknown of death, one strikingly human task always remains: what is to be done with the remains of those whom Mother Earth has called home?

UPWARD SUN RIVER MOUTH CHILD

The archaeological evidence for human habitation in North America is one of my personal favorite topics within the field. Thanks to the collaborative work of both Indigenous and non-Indigenous researchers, the peopling of North America is a topic whose mysteries are being unraveled faster than ever before. While much of the lives of Paleo-Indigenous peoples remains shrouded in mystery, the Xaasaa Na' archaeological site in what is now known as Alaska has shed a unique window onto life and death some 11,500 years ago.

In the Tanana River Valley, archaeologists discovered the remains of several infants that had been buried in what had once been a small village. Two tiny and fragile remains were found at the bottom of what had once been a multipurpose hearth. The bottom of the pit contained two small skeletons: one believed to be around twelve weeks old and the other who was likely stillborn. With them were traces of red ocher, a material used as far as Maine by the Paleo-Indigenous Red Paint People. There were also four antler artifacts that appear to have been painted in this red mineral. Oddly, the DNA analysis of these two infants suggests that the two did not share the same mother, despite being in the same grave. A second house tells another tragic story. On top of layers of ash, plant material, and bones that had been buried in an in-home refuse pit/ hearth were found the cremated remains of a three-year-old child. It seems the toddler was buried in the pit and the home abandoned quickly afterward.

These instances are two that are as tragic as they are fascinating. The inclusion of two unrelated individuals within the same grave would indicate that the people who inhabited this inhospitable region at the end of the last glacial maximum had a complex and intertwined social structure. The three-year-old, however, particularly captivated archaeologists. It tells a story of more than just burial practices, but the very human story of loss. Our imaginations can piece together the story of tragedy that befell this ancient family who left their child buried beneath their hearth as they abandoned their home. This part of the story has captivated

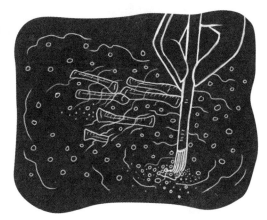

researchers so much that the child was even given a name in the local language—Xaasaa Cheege Ts'eniin: the Upward Sun River Mouth Child.

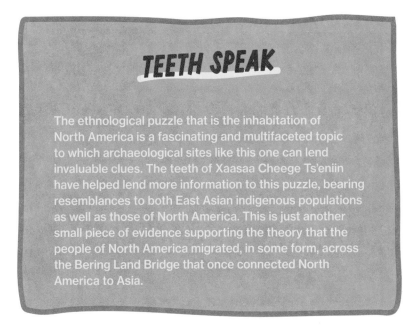

TEETH SPEAK

The ethnological puzzle that is the inhabitation of North America is a fascinating and multifaceted topic to which archaeological sites like this one can lend invaluable clues. The teeth of Xaasaa Cheege Ts'eniin have helped lend more information to this puzzle, bearing resemblances to both East Asian indigenous populations as well as those of North America. This is just another small piece of evidence supporting the theory that the people of North America migrated, in some form, across the Bering Land Bridge that once connected North America to Asia.

TILL DEATH DO US PART . . .
AND THEN SOME

For a couple to be buried next to each other is a fairly common practice. Modern graveyards are full of plots containing the names of partners as well as entire families in larger plots. But love, being a constant human emotion, has found itself wrapped in the dark embrace of death many times throughout history. Six thousand years ago, fate would reach out its hands to a couple who, to this day, find themselves wrapped in one another's arms in a symbol of eternal love in the cold face of death.

The Lovers of Valdaro is one of the most famous burials from the European region, due to the spectacular preservation and unique position of this couple. The pair were discovered in 2007 in Valdaro, near the city of Mantua, in Italy. The discovery was stunning, consisting of two individuals with faces positioned within inches of each other and their arms intertwined, draped over one another in a lover's embrace. Analysis of the skeletons indicated that the pair were a man and woman and were likely around the age of twenty at the time of death. Beyond the initial shock of the position of the Neolithic pair, archaeologists also discovered several flint tools, including an arrowhead positioned behind the male's neck and a flint knife by the woman's thigh.

The initial conclusion for how they met their death was a violent one

THE ENCYCLOPEDIA OF THE WEIRD AND WONDERFUL

caused by the flint weapon heads positioned around them. However, analysis indicated that this was unlikely as no skeletal evidence of violence was found on the pair. It is far more likely that these flint tools were included as grave goods, a practice that would have been consistent with many other burial rites from this time period and region. The second option was that the pair died this way, perhaps freezing to death while huddling for warmth. This was also ruled out as the deliberate position of the bodies is more in line with artificial placement than the natural positions that two people would assume. While nothing is known about these two today, the tender burial conjures forth the image of a pair of star-crossed lovers, who, even in the face of death, will spend an eternity in each other's arms.

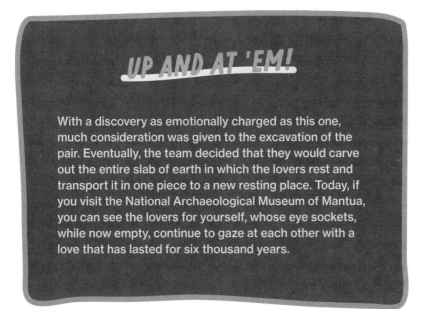

UP AND AT 'EM!

With a discovery as emotionally charged as this one, much consideration was given to the excavation of the pair. Eventually, the team decided that they would carve out the entire slab of earth in which the lovers rest and transport it in one piece to a new resting place. Today, if you visit the National Archaeological Museum of Mantua, you can see the lovers for yourself, whose eye sockets, while now empty, continue to gaze at each other with a love that has lasted for six thousand years.

DEATH STANDING

Most burial customs that involve interring the dead in the ground have one major thing in common. Graves, for the most part, involve the deceased buried lying flat, either on their back, side, or curled in the fetal position. But a Mesolithic grave site discovered in what is today Germany sheds light on an unusual burial custom from a group of people that lived there some six thousand years ago. In 2012, archaeologists working in Brandenburg, Germany, set their sights on an ancient graveyard that was discovered during a dig in the early 1960s. This new dig aimed to excavate some of the new and previously unresearched burials. One site caught attention: a smudge of black earth that stood out from its surroundings. Believed to be a fire pit at first, excavation found the remains of a man buried just 2 feet (0.6 m) beneath.

The man's bones were found in a disarticulated heap. The skull, ribs, and arms were all accounted for. The spine was of particular interest,

with the lower vertebrae in order. Among these bones were thirty flint grave goods. However, as researchers dug deeper they discovered that the man's lower legs and feet were fully articulated and positioned vertically within the soil horizon. This suggested that the man had been buried in a standing position up to his knees or thighs, and left to the mercy of the elements after his death. The pit that he was

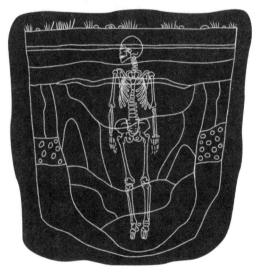

positioned in bears a different composition than the soil around it and seems to have been filled in with sand. The researchers' hypothesis was supported further by the evidence of damage on the upper part of his body caused by the teeth of scavenging animals.

The man belonged to a culture that today we know little about, making it hard to determine the significance of this burial. What we do know is that he was in his mid-twenties at the time of death, and minimal wear on his skeleton, as well as the presence of many flint artifacts, suggests that he may have been a craftsman. The significance of this type of burial is not concretely known, but echoes similarities with other parts of the world that believe in returning the body to nature through exposure to the elements. While we may never know exactly why this man was buried like this, it conjures a macabre yet poetic image of the process of returning to the earth.

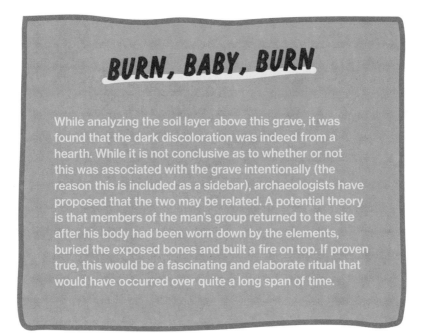

BURN, BABY, BURN

While analyzing the soil layer above this grave, it was found that the dark discoloration was indeed from a hearth. While it is not conclusive as to whether or not this was associated with the grave intentionally (the reason this is included as a sidebar), archaeologists have proposed that the two may be related. A potential theory is that members of the man's group returned to the site after his body had been worn down by the elements, buried the exposed bones and built a fire on top. If proven true, this would be a fascinating and elaborate ritual that would have occurred over quite a long span of time.

THE SPIRAL BURIAL

Understanding the burial practices of ancient peoples can be as confusing as it is fascinating. As one delves further back into our past, graves become few and far between, and with no living individuals to explain the oddities of ancient burials it is up to archaeologists to parse together their meanings from sparse evidence. Despite all the information we have to work with, some graves can still leave archaeologists scratching their heads, such as the unusual spiral grave discovered in the modern country of Mexico.

The streets of Mexico City are paved over thousands of years of human history, making them a treasure trove whenever work is done. It was just one of these construction projects at the Pontifical University of Mexico that yielded the remains of ten individuals arranged in a 6½ foot (2 m) spiral. The deceased were both male and female and had a wide range of ages from adults to teenagers and even an infant and a toddler. Along with the dead were a handful of pottery fragments from long broken ceramic vessels that had been included as grave goods. Among the dead were some with signs of body modifications. Several of the individuals had their teeth filed, a custom that exists in many different parts of the world, and more drastically two of the individuals showed the obvious signs of Mesoamerica's most famous anatomical alterations: skull elongation from binding.

The direct causes of death for these individuals has yet to be identified, which has left archaeologists with a puzzle. The burial dates to about 2,500 years ago and is attributed to the settlement of Tlalpan, which far predates the more famous civilization of the Aztecs that would later arise in this mountain basin. The significance of the spiral, while hotly contested, has been hypothesized to be of some symbolic importance. Just one of these theories is that the burial shows the stages of life, a cyclical shape made up of individuals who met their ends at various points in their lives. It is likely that we may never know the exact reason for this burial, but it is both haunting and intriguing to imagine the ceremony that took place on this spot more than two thousand years ago.

SKULL BINDING

From Africa to South America, countless cultures around the world have practiced a type of body modification known officially as artificial cranial deformation, or more colloquially: skull binding. The practice begins when an individual is still an infant, leaving the plates of the skull pliable. From here, binding can occur with cloth, rope, or any other sort of binding agent. Over time, the skull would shape to the outside pressure, and the eventually hardened bones would retain the elongated form. Unfortunately, today much of the popularity of elongated skulls comes from pseudoscientists who claim them to be either inspired by extraterrestrials or, for the more insane, actual skulls of extraterrestrials. It may come as a shocker, but they are not extraterrestrials.

NGABEN

Fire is perceived as a purifying force in many places around the world. A terrifying source of chaos at its worst, and an agent of safety and security at its best. It is no small wonder that the purification brought on by a scorching inferno is one that has, for thousands of years, been used in burial rituals. A unique cremation custom that exists within the Hindu Balinese group is known as *ngaben* and is one of the most important ceremonies within the culture.

During this funerary custom, the remains of the deceased are placed inside a *patulangan*, or wooden casket, around which is constructed a massive figure of a bull. Occasionally these pyres will also take the form of a cow, lion, elephant, or deer, should a different animal be deemed more fitting for the age, gender, and social class of the deceased interred within. The only real rule is that the construction must be of an animal with four legs. This is a symbolic gesture to the *kanda empat*, four siblings within local mythology. On top of this, there may be constructed a *wadah*; an enormous (up to 60 feet/18 m!) tall tower built in an Indonesian pagoda style that acts as a symbol of the prestige of the deceased. When the time comes, the entire structure is set ablaze by a priest bearing a blessed torch.

This process carries with it myriad religious and spiritual significance. The entire process is a celebration, rather than a grieving ceremony, being seen by those who practice it to help shepherd the soul of the deceased to heaven. It is even encouraged to not cry at the event, as this is seen as something that could add difficulty along the soul's path. The Hindu Balinese believe that the body is merely a mortal catalyst. As such it is seen that with the destruction of the body comes the opportunity for the soul to proceed unencumbered to the great beyond.

A BIG SEND-OFF

On July 15, 2008, Bali hosted its largest ngaben celebration in nearly thirty years. The event was a sendoff for Tjokorada Gde Agung Suyasa, a member of the royal family and lifelong supporter of the island's traditional cultures. As a result, the celebration of his life that took place at his cremation saw a crowd that is estimated to have ranged in the hundred thousands. In the city of Ubud, groups of 250 men worked in a relay to transport a nearly 100-foot (30 m) tower to the cremation site. It was there that Suyasa, interred in a spectacular black-bull sarcophagus, was released from the mortal realm in a blaze fit for royalty.

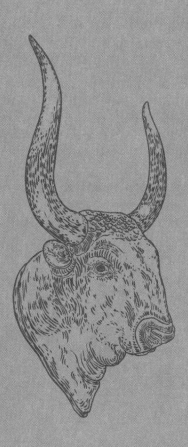

FAMADIHANA

Regardless of one's views on death, and about celebration or mourning, one of the most challenging parts of it for those of us who remain on this Earth is the inability to tell our lost loved ones about all that they have missed. It can feel bittersweet that some of those to whom we were close to for much of our lives cannot be there to experience major life milestones with us, such as celebrating new jobs, marriages, or the births of children. But on the island of Madagascar, the Malagasy people have found a solution to this dilemma through a ceremony called "the turning of the bones."

Famadihana, as it is called in the local language, is a celebration of the lives of the deceased and an opportunity to share the joys of life with them once again. During the celebration, everyone, including both immediate family and extended relatives, gather to exhume the remains of their deceased ancestors. During the festivities that follow, the deceased are given new shrouds and introduced to new members of the family. They are also given gifts of things that they enjoyed in life, everything from money to alcohol to even being spritzed with their favorite perfumes! Each Famadihana, which can be separated by upward of five years, is not a time of grieving, but of celebration. Family members brought together through this event have a celebration more akin to a family reunion than a funeral.

The groups that traditionally celebrate Famadihana believe that there are two states within the social system: you are either living or an ancestor. The dead, before their first exhumation, are neither of these and are buried in a temporary tomb until the first time they are exhumed. The point when the first exhumation happens typically occurs when the spirit of the interred appears to a family elder in a dream and tells them that they are cold and need new clothes. This spurs on the first removal of the remains from the tomb and their welcoming into the rank of an ancestor.

THE THREE TYPES OF FAMADIHANA

The groups that practice this unique celebration of life have three distinct customs that fall under the Famadihana umbrella. The first is the need to move the deceased to their ancestral city. This is seen as an important rite and many families work to have their family plots in their ancestors' places of origin. The second, and most common, is dressing the deceased in new silk robes. This is a ceremony that occurs at odd years, typically five to seven, after the last re-dressing. And the third and final rite is the moving of the ancestors to a new tomb. This can happen because a tomb has sustained damage, but some tombs are intentionally unfinished in accordance with Malagasy beliefs that before the first exhumation, the deceased are in an in-between state.

THE TOMB OF THE UNKNOWN SOLDIER

The honoring of military dead is a practice as ancient as warfare itself. The catastrophic loss of life caused by warfare leaves those who survive with a profound combination of grief, horror, and guilt. Because of this, humankind has long practiced elaborate burials for our honored dead, elevating them to near deification through celebration and burial that uplifts them and the ultimate sacrifice they made. The modern age is no different, and Arlington National Cemetery is home to one of the most famous modern ceremonial military graves in the world. The Tomb of the Unknown Soldier is a place of reflection and reverence within this cemetery in Arlington, Virginia, USA. It is a large, white, marble sarcophagus decorated with Beaux-Arts and neoclassical motifs. The exterior of it contains a facade depicting three individuals: Peace, Valor, and Victory.

Within the tomb are the remains of three unknown individuals who fought and died with the United States military throughout the last hundred years. The tomb was originally constructed as a monument to the catastrophic loss of life caused by World War I and was intended to house the remains of one of the countless unidentified American dead who littered the cemeteries and mass graves of Europe. The remains of the Unknown Soldier were exhumed from a cemetery in France and transported back home to the United States to be interred on November 11, 1921. Since this construction, Unknown Soldiers from World War II, the Korean War, and the Vietnam War have been added in separate crypts as part of the memorial plaza.

Today, the Tomb of the Unknown Soldier is patrolled around the clock by the 3rd US Infantry Regiment. Referred to as "The Old Guard," the 3rd US Infantry has guarded the tomb nonstop since 1937. The guards are picked carefully and the routine they follow is meticulous, following a highly specific series of motions as they patrol the front of the marble sarcophagus. The remains inside the tomb will likely never be identified, but in their lack of personal identity they have found a new place within the national identity, forever lying beneath the marble slab that reads:

"HERE RESTS IN
HONORED GLORY
AN AMERICAN
SOLDIER
KNOWN BUT TO GOD."

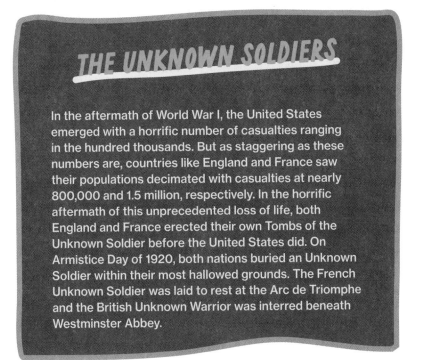

THE UNKNOWN SOLDIERS

In the aftermath of World War I, the United States emerged with a horrific number of casualties ranging in the hundred thousands. But as staggering as these numbers are, countries like England and France saw their populations decimated with casualties at nearly 800,000 and 1.5 million, respectively. In the horrific aftermath of this unprecedented loss of life, both England and France erected their own Tombs of the Unknown Soldier before the United States did. On Armistice Day of 1920, both nations buried an Unknown Soldier within their most hallowed grounds. The French Unknown Soldier was laid to rest at the Arc de Triomphe and the British Unknown Warrior was interred beneath Westminster Abbey.

ABEBU ADEKAI

In the Western world, death is frequently viewed as a unilateral tragedy and one that can only be adequately observed through mourning and quiet respect. However, this is not the case everywhere, and many cultures have found death to be an opportunity to explore the more celebratory aspects of life through art and expression. One of these that has gained notable internet popularity in recent years is the *abebu adekai* coffins from the country of Ghana.

The name itself translates to "boxes with proverbs" and is a unique form of artistic expression that began to arise in the 1950s. Among the Ga people, this tradition began to gain a foothold of popularity. The process is one that is nothing short of visually spectacular, involving the creation of coffins that look more like large sculptures. These abebu adekai can be shaped as anything, from cars to Coke bottles to fruit to animals and even, in my personal favorite examples, to airplanes and Nokia cell phones. The inspiration for these coffins comes directly from the life of the individual being buried in it. Artists, family members, and even forward-thinking pre-deceaseds, will work to create an abebu adekai that draws on elements from the passions, careers, and hobbies of the person who will be in it. As a result, the deceased can quite literally take their favorite things to the grave.

In recent years the advent of the internet has propelled this unique tradition into the limelight around the world, with countless people stumbling upon these personality-filled coffins in their online escapades. Thanks to this sudden spotlight, the works of the Ghanaian artists who make these pieces of art have found a market among artist communities, with some displayed in museums around the world. Because of the spike in attention, artists have been able to hone their craft even further, adopting new techniques and methods to create ever more elaborate and entertaining celebrations of life.

HUMBLE BEGINNINGS

Most of the traditions discussed in this book have a shockingly long history, but the tradition of abebu adekai is one that is actually fairly new to the world stage. The craft was pioneered by Seth Kane Kwei in the 1950s. The story goes that Kwei was commissioned to make a palanquin, a seat on which chiefs are carried, in the shape of a cocoa pod. As fate would have it, the commissioning chief passed away before being able to use it. For some reason, it was decided to bury him in the cocoa pod instead, much to the delight of the funeral-goers. And abebu adekai was born! While the great Kwei is no longer in this mortal realm, his carpentry workshop still bears his name, and his dream is kept alive by the workers who still produce these elaborate coffins there today.

GOING GREEN

In the United States, the first steps of a funeral can resemble a construction project more than a celebration of life. By the time most people find themselves six feet under, they are also surrounded by a massive sarcophagus made of concrete and rebar, an inner liner, an enormous metal coffin, and have been pumped full of more preservatives than a Twinkie. Needless to say, many in the modern world are shying away from these traditions that are not only a massively wasteful and expensive process, but a bit of a macabre perspective for the final resting place of one's mortal remains. For this reason, today many are turning toward green burials.

A green burial is a blanket term that covers burials with far more biodegradable aspects. Deceased who are given a green burial have their body wrapped in a biodegradable fabric before typically being interred in a simple wooden box, some of which don't even contain nails. Along with this, the body remains unpreserved, allowing it to decompose in a natural way and return to the earth along with the box it is buried in. These funerals can vary greatly but some venues will plant a tree of choice along with the dead, allowing the mortal remains of the deceased to give life to new growth. This results in a towering memorial forest rather than a sea of manicured grass and polished granite headstones.

While it may not seem all that different from a traditional burial, the effect it has on the world is drastic. The construction of a reinforced burial tomb releases as much carbon dioxide as a 500-mile (805 km) car drive. Furthermore, the full impact of traditional burials when fully combined is staggering. In the course of a year, Americans bury more than 1.5 million tons (1.4 Mg) of concrete, 70 thousand tons (63,503 Mg) of steel, 20 million board feet (47,195 m³) of wood, and, most nauseatingly, nearly 4.5 million gallons (17 million L) of embalming fluid. The antiseptic and industrial nature of these burials has turned the stomachs of many and prompted a shift away from this highly intrusive tradition. Nearly 55 percent of Americans now say that they would entertain the idea of a green burial, noting a striking shift toward this economic, environmental, and respectful method of laying the dead to rest.

WITHIN THE WILDFLOWERS

For most of this book, I have tried to follow a chronological order, with older entries being at the beginning and progressing through time to the modern world. But here, in our last entry, I would like to break this trend. Because here at the end, we are going back. Way back.

Before the tomb of the Unknown Soldier was constructed, before a case of French champagne slipped beneath the waves on a doomed merchant ship, before Romans tried to heal all ills with cabbage, and the people of Pentecost Island flung themselves from wooden towers. We are going back 45,000 years. Back to a time when the world was blanketed in ancient forests and the night sky was peppered with countless stars that splashed across the heavens like diamond dust.

They sought shelter in the maw of a cave perched high on a mountain top. The valley below was a carpet of color, rich blue cornflowers glowing against a sea of white yarrow. The pink blossoms of delicate hollyhocks swayed alongside the prickly sabers that protected the golden bloom of the thistles and the breeze that danced through them was laced with the smell of hyacinths. Through the bottom of the valley ran a river, a hard stroke of blue speckled with the ever-shifting white gleams of sunlight that showered the valley in its heavenly glow.

They were much like us. They lived with their family members. Cared for the sick and injured. Laughed at each other's jokes and captivated each other with tales by firelight. In nearly all ways they were like us— save one. A tiny genetic difference, infinitesimal in the grand scheme of things, but enough to set them apart from us as our relatives *Homo neanderthalensis*. And it was from this bastion in the mountains that they lived their lives and laid their heads at night. But they, like us, share one commonality with every living creature that has ever blossomed forth from this planet. Someday, we are all called home.

It was warm the day he died. Whether or not anyone was with him when he passed, we don't know. Perhaps he was in the presence of family or friends. Perhaps the members of his community cried as they dug his grave. Or maybe they laughed and told stories of his life. They may have come together for a meal, or a song, or perhaps they just sat in silence as the emptiness of grief filled them. But what

we do know is that someone ventured out from the cave mouth and into the meadow below. That someone may have been his friend, his partner, or his child. There, on a canvas of color painted by Mother Earth herself, this someone picked flowers.

Back in the cave, a hole was dug in the ground on which he had once walked. The friend, or spouse, or child returned, arms filled with a gift to the dead. It was there, in an unmarked grave high in the mountains that the man was laid to rest on a bed of wildflowers. And as dirt covered the pink hollyhocks, the white yarrow, and the prickly golden thistles, a breeze splashed through the cave's mouth, rich with the unmistakable smell of hyacinths.

On the day in 1960 that Shanidar 4, known colloquially as the flower burial, was discovered, someone else was buried with flowers. Perhaps they were someone's grandparent or a childhood friend. A colleague, neighbor, or child. Their name and story are known only to those who knew them, yet the mourning these people felt as the steel casket was lowered into the ground is a bitter sting that is all too familiar to many.

THE ENCYCLOPEDIA OF THE WEIRD AND WONDERFUL

At the same time this was happening, on the other side of the world or in the next town over, a child was brought into the world. Kicking and screaming as anyone would be when faced with the harsh reality of *reality*, they got a little slap on the feet, a tiny hat, and their very own name. The next day they were home in the hands of their relieved yet exhausted parents, who found themselves inundated with gifts and a bouquet of flowers. Where that child is today, who knows? Perhaps they are a teacher or an architect. A musician or a miner. A parent or a grandparent. Or perhaps it's you. You are sitting here right now, reading a book about the sacred cycle of life that we are all part of.

From here, the book is yours to write. You are the newest entry in a story that never ends. You are a triumph of nature. A physical memory of all who came before you. A product of a planet that has ensured you the ability to be here right now. I have no words to say how incredible your existence is.

Go jump in a puddle or climb a tree. Open a book or go out to the movies. Hike a mountain or swim in a stream. Call your mother and tell her you love her.

Live fully.

Feel deeply.

Love unapologetically.

You are the single greatest miracle the Earth has ever produced.

The pen is in your hands now.

What will you write?

REFERENCES

THE EARLY YEARS

Cohen, Jennie. "Prehistoric Children Finger-Painted on Cave Walls." History, A&E Television Networks. Last updated 22 August 2018, https://www.history.com/news/prehistoric-children-finger-painted-on-cave-walls.

Dagonell the Juggler. "Hopscotch: A History." 1 November 2005, https://www.albany.edu/~sw7656.

Dunne, J., et al. "Milk of Ruminants in Ceramic Baby Bottles from Prehistoric Child Graves." *Nature*, 574, 246-248 (2019). https://www.nature.com/articles/s41586-019-1572-x.

Faris, Peter. "Giant Beavers in Native American Culture and Art." *Academia.edu*. 23 September 2019. https://www.academia.edu/40424394/GIANT_BEAVERS_IN_NATIVE_AMERICAN_CULTURE_AND_ART.

Ford, Toni Marie. "The History of The Barbie Doll." The Culture Trip. 19 March 2016. https://theculturetrip.com/north-america/usa/articles/the-history-of-the-barbie-doll/.

Gamesver. "Hopscotch (Game) 101: History, Origins, Gameplay, Variations ..." *Gamesver*. Accessed 23 January 2023. https://www.gamesver.com/hopscotch-game-101-history-origins-gameplay-variations.

Gorman, James. "Prehistoric Parents Used Baby Bottles Made of Pottery." *The New York Times*. Last updated 1 October 2019. https://www.nytimes.com/2019/09/25/science/prehistoric-baby-bottles.html.

Handwerk, Brian. "Bronze Age Baby Bottles Reveal How Some Ancient Infants Were Fed." *Smithsonian Magazine*. 25 September 2019. https://www.smithsonianmag.com/science-nature/bronze-age-baby-bottles-reveal-how-ancient-infants-were-fed-180973210.

Heyworth, Robin. "Mesoamerican Wheeled Toys." *Uncovered History*. 18 July 2015. https://uncoveredhistory.com/mesoamerica/wheeled-toys.

Holland, Brynn. "Barbie through the Ages." History, A&E Television Networks. 29 January 2016. https://www.history.com/news/barbie-through-the-ages.

Lanese, Nicoletta. "Kids' Fossilized Handprints May Be Some of the World's Oldest Art." *Scientific American*. 21 September 2021. https://www.scientificamerican.com/article/kids-fossilized-handprints-may-be-some-of-the-worlds-oldest-art.

Lord, M.G. "Barbie." In *Encyclopædia Britannica*, online ed., last updated 11 June 2021. https://www.britannica.com/topic/Barbie.

Mailar, Sahana. "Hopscotch Game: Everything You'd Want to Know!" *Hopscotch*. 11 December 2019. https://www.hopscotch.in/blog/hopscotch-game-everything-you-would-want-to-know.

Marshall, Michael. "Why Humans Have Evolved to Drink Milk." *BBC Future*, British Broadcasting Corporation (BBC). 19 February 2019. https://www.bbc.com/future/article/20190218-when-did-humans-start-drinking-cows-milk.

Minnesota Department of Natural Resources. "Ruppia Cirrhosa (Spiral Ditchgrass)." *Rare Species Guide*. Accessed 23 January 2023. https://www.dnr.state.mn.us/rsg/profile.html?action=elementDetail&selectedElement=PMRUP01020.

Muzdakis, Madeleine. "4,000-Year-Old Ancient Egyptian Writing Board Shows Student's Spelling Mistakes with Teacher's Corrections." *My Modern Met*. 5 May 2021. https://mymodernmet.com/ancient-egyptian-students-writing-board.

National Park Service. "White Sands, National Park of New Mexico: Plants." Accessed 23 January 2023. https://www.nps.gov/whsa/learn/nature/plants.htm.

Philippsen, Bente. "The Freshwater Reservoir Effect in Radiocarbon Dating." *Heritage Science*, 1, 24 (2013). https://heritagesciencejournal.springeropen.com/articles/10.1186/2050-7445-1-24.

ProCon. "Lactose Intolerance by Country." *ProCon*, part of the Britannica Group. Last updated 25 July 2022. https://milk.procon.org/lactose-intolerance-by-country.

Smith, Justine E.H. "Onfim Wuz Here: On the Unlikely Art of a Medieval Russian Boy." *Literary Hub*. 26 February 2018. https://lithub.com/onfim-wuz-here-on-the-unlikely-art-of-a-medieval-russian-boy.

Wickenden, Paul. "The Art of Onfim: Medieval Novgorod through the Eyes of a Child." Accessed 23 January 2023. https://www.goldschp.net/SIG/onfim/onfim.html.

Zubchuk, Tamara. "4,000 Year Old Children's Rattle Beautifully Crafted as Bear Cub's Head: And It Still Rattles!" *The Siberian Times*. 21 October 2016. https://siberiantimes.com/science/others/news/n0780-4000-year-old-childrens-rattle-beautifully-crafted-as-bear-cubs-head-and-it-still-rattles.

EAT, DRINK, AND BE MERRY

Allen, Ike. "Cuy." *Atlas Obscura*. Accessed 23 January 2023. https://www.atlasobscura.com/foods/cuy-guinea-pig.

British Broadcasting Corporation (BBC). "Chinese Archaeologists Unearth 2,400-Year-Old 'Soup'." *BBC News*. 13 December 2020. https://www.bbc.com/news/world-asia-pacific-11981666.

Cascone, Sarah. "An Ancient Fast Food Restaurant in Pompeii That Served Honey-Roasted Rodents Is Now Open to the Public." *Artnet News*. 13 August 2021. https://news.artnet.com/art-world/pompeii-opens-recently-discovered-ancient-fast-food-restaurant-1998265.

Geiling, Natasha. "The Widow Who Created the Champagne Industry." *Smithsonian Magazine*. 5 November 2013. https://www.smithsonianmag.com/arts-culture/the-widow-who-created-the-champagne-industry-180947570.

Grahn, Emma. "Keeping your (food) cool: From ice harvesting to electric refrigeration." O Say Can You See?: Stories from the Museum (blog). 29 April 2015. https://americanhistory.si.edu/blog/ice-harvesting-electric-refrigeration.

Harford, Tim. "How refrigeration revolutionised global trade." BBC. 20 November 2017. https://www.bbc.com/news/business-41902071.

Hoffman, Adam. "170-Year-Old Champagne Recovered (and Tasted) from a Baltic Shipwreck." *Smithsonian Magazine*. 20 April 2015. https://www.smithsonianmag.com/science-nature/170-year-old-champagne-recovered-and-tasted-baltic-shipwreck-180955050.

Hosseini, Bahreh, and Ali Namazian. "An Overview of Iranian Ice Repositories, an Example of Traditional Indigenous Architecture." *METU Journal of the Faculty of Architecture*, 29, no. 2 (2012): 223-234. http://jfa.arch.metu.edu.tr/archive/0258-5316/2012/cilt29/sayi_2/223-234.pdf.

Kudrich, Chris. "Guinea Pig Last Supper." *Atlas Obscura*. Accessed 23 January 2023. https://www.atlasobscura.com/places/guinea-pig-last-supper.

Lowry, Brad. "Kiviak, Greenland Inuit Fermented Seal Dish." *The Foodie Blog.* Accessed 23 January 2023. https://www.culinaryschools.org/blog/kiviak-greenland-inuit-fermented-seal-dish.

Mac, Andrea G. "Beondegi." *Atlas Obscura.* Accessed 23 January 2023. https://www.atlasobscura.com/foods/beondegi-silkworm-pupae-korea.

Master Blaster (Steven Le Blanc, Masami M). "Bat Soup in Palau Is Pretty Intense." SoraNews24. 11 November 2017. https://soranews24.com/2017/11/11/bat-soup-in-palau-is-pretty-intense.

Moseley-Williams, Sorrel. "The One Dish to Try in Peru Is . . . Guinea Pig." *Condé Nast Traveler.* 25 September 2014. https://www.cntraveler.com/stories/2014-09-25/the-one-dish-to-try-in-peru-is-guinea-pig.

Oxner, Reese. "What's on the Menu in Ancient Pompeii? Duck, Goat, Snail, Researchers Say." National Public Radio (NPR). 27 December 2020. https://www.npr.org/2020/12/27/950645473/whats-on-the-menu-in-ancient-pompeii-duck-goat-snail-researchers-say.

Tarantola, Andrew. "This Inuit Delicacy Is the Turducken from Hell." *Gizmodo.* 15 February 2012. https://gizmodo.com/this-inuit-delicacy-is-the-turducken-from-hell-5885202.

TasteAtlas. "Fruit Bat Soup." TasteAtlas. Accessed 23 January 2023. https://www.tasteatlas.com/fruit-bat-soup.

Usher, Charles. "Salty Silkworm Pupae Are the One Street Food You Shouldn't Miss in South Korea." Matador Network. 17 April 2022. https://matadornetwork.com/read/beondegi.

Ward, Charlotte. "10 Of the Oldest Foods Ever Discovered." *History Hit.* 28 January 2022. https://www.historyhit.com/oldest-foods-ever-discovered.

Warner, Andrew. "This Is How Bologna Is Really Made." *Mashed.* Last updated 15 April 2022. https://www.mashed.com/193323/this-is-how-bologna-is-really-made.

Zagorsky, Jay. "POV: The 100th Anniversary of Prohibition Reminds Us that Bans Rarely Work." *BU Today* part of Boston University. 17 January 2020. https://www.bu.edu/articles/2020/pov-the-100th-anniversary-of-prohibition-reminds-us-that-bans-rarely-work.

OUR BEST FRIENDS

Bieniek, Adam. "Cher Ami: The Pigeon That Saved the Lost Battalion." The United States World War One Centennial Commission. Accessed 23 January 2023. https://www.worldwar1centennial.org/index.php/communicate/press-media/wwi-centennial-news/1210-cher-ami-the-pigeon-that-saved-the-lost-battalion.html.

Crowfoot, G. M., and N. de G. Davies. "The Tunic of Tut'ankhamūn." *The Journal of Egyptian Archaeology*, vol. 27 (1941): 113–30. https://journals.sagepub.com/doi/abs/10.1177/030751334102700112.

Day, Leslie Preston. "Dog Burials in the Greek World." *American Journal of Archaeology* 88, no. 1 (1984): 21–32. https://doi.org/10.2307/504595.

Dog Breed Info. "Tesem." Dog Breed Info. Accessed 23 January 2023. https://www.dogbreedinfo.com/t/tesem.htm.

Dzikiewicz, Kate, and Paul Griswold Howes Fellow. "Old Rip, Miracle Horned Toad." RoadsideAmerica. Accessed 23 January 2023. https://www.roadsideamerica.com/story/3631.

Gilleland, Micheal. "Ancient Dog Epitaphs." *Laudator Temporis Acti* (blog). 11 May 2006, https://laudatortemporisacti.blogspot.com/2006/05/ancient-dog-epitaphs.html.

Harris, Karen. "Ancient Dog Tombs: Greek/Roman Epitaphs, Funerals, & Quotes about Dead Pets." History Daily. 19 September 2020. https://historydaily.org/ancient-dog-tombs-greek-roman-epitaphs-funerals-quotes-about-dead-pets/2.

Henry Cowls. "War Pigeon." 7 November 2019. https://www.henrycowls.net/blog-en/war-pigeon.html.

Kruschwitz, Peter. "Every Dog Has His Day." *The Petrified Muse* (blog). 20 June 2015. https://thepetrifiedmuse.blog/2015/06/20/every-dog-has-his-day.

MacDonald, James. "For Pets in Ancient Egypt, Life was Hard (or Really Easy)." JSTOR Daily. 1 July 2015. https://daily.jstor.org/pets-ancient-egypt-life-hard-really-easy.

Merkelbach, Reinhold, and Josef Stauber. *Steinepigramme aus dem griechischen Osten*. Munich/Leipzig: B.G. Teubner, 1998-2004.

National Purebred Dog Day®. "What Breed Was Abuwtiyuw, One of the First Dogs Whose Name We Know?" National Purebred Dog Day®. 29 June 2017. https://nationalpurebreddogday.com/what-breed-was-abuwtiyuw-one-of-the-first-dogs-whose-name-we-know.

Osypinska, Marta, Michał Skibniewski, and Piotr Osypinski. "Ancient Pets. The Health, Diet and Diversity of Cats, Dogs and Monkeys from the Red Sea Port of Berenice (Egypt) in the 1st-2nd centuries AD." *World Archaeology*, 52, no. 4 (2021): 639-653. https://doi.org/10.1080/00438243.2020.1870545.

Reisner, George A. "Digital Giza Library." Digital Giza, part of the Giza Project at Harvard University. Accessed 23 January 2023. http://giza.fas.harvard.edu/library.

Reisner, George A. "The Dog Which Was Honored by the King of Upper and Lower Egypt." *Bulletin of the Museum of Fine Arts* 34, no. 206 (1936): 96–99. http://www.jstor.org/stable/4170605.

Smith, Gordon, and Frank Hales. "World War 1 at Sea – In Memory of Skipper Thomas Crisp VC, DSC RNR and the Hales Naval Family." Accessed 31 March 2023. https://www.naval-history.net/WW1Memoir-Hales.htm.

Stephanie Little Wolf. "Precolumbian Tribal Dogs in the Americas." Sled Dog Central. Accessed 23 January 2023. https://www.sleddogcentral.com/features/little_wolf/precolumbian.htm.

Tarlach, Gemma. "Is This Egyptian Site the World's Oldest Pet Cemetery?" *Atlas Obscura*. 4 March 2021. https://www.atlasobscura.com/articles/oldest-pet-cemetery-berenice-egypt.

The American University in Cairo. "King Tut's Sandals Featured at Ancient Egyptian Footwear Exhibition." The American University in Cairo. 11 October 2015. https://www.aucegypt.edu/news/stories/king-tuts-sandals-featured-ancient-egyptian-footwear-exhibition.

The Bruce Museum. "The Tragedy of the Most Hated Bird in America." *Storage Room No. 2*. 17 April 2017. http://www.storagetwo.com/blog/2017/4/the-tragedy-of-the-most-hated-bird-in-america.

Viegas, Jennifer. "Prehistoric Dog Lived, Died among Humans." National Broadcasting Company (NBC). 28 February 2011. https://www.nbcnews.com/id/wbna41830341.

United Nations Educational, Scientific and Cultural Organization (UNESCO). "Lake Baikal." UNESCO. Accessed 23 January 2023. https://whc.unesco.org/en/list/754.

Wood, Patsy. "Saved by a Pigeon." Golden Gate Audobon Society. 3 May 2022. https://goldengateaudubon.org/blog-posts/savedbypigeons.

Worldly Dogs. "Tesem: Egyptian Hunting Dog." Worldly Dogs. Accessed 23 January 2023. https://www.worldlydogs.com/tesem.html.

PLAY AND LEISURE

"Ancient North Americans Played High-Stakes Games." Ancient Origins®. Last updated 6 August 2012. https://www.ancient-origins.net/history-ancient-traditions/ancient-north-americans-played-high-stakes-games-009568.

Azéma, Marc, and Florent Rivère. "Animation in Palaeolithic art: A pre-echo of cinema." *Antiquity*, 86, no. 332 (June 2012): 316-324. https://doi.org/10.1017/S0003598X00062785.

Claydon, Jane, Ed. "Origin & History." World Lacrosse™. Accessed 23 January 2023. https://worldlacrosse.sport/about/origin-history.

"How to Play Bao." UltraBoardGames. Accessed 23 January 2023. https://www.ultraboardgames.com/mancala/bao.php.

"How to Play Pallanguzhi Board Game (Origin, Variants, Components)." Toys for Kids Reviews. 26 December 2019. https://toysinindia.com/pallanguzhi-board-game-origin-variants-components.

"Mū Tōrere." DBpedia. Accessed 23 January 2023. https://dbpedia.org/page/M%C5%AB_t%C5%8Drere.

Narodni Muzej Slovenije (National Museum of Slovenia). "Neanderthal Flute." National Museum of Slovenia. Accessed 23 January 2023. https://www.nms.si/en/collections/highlights/343-Neanderthal-flute.

Sirani, Jordan. "The 10 Best-Selling Video Games of All Time." IGN. Last updated 17 December 2022. https://www.ign.com/articles/best-selling-video-games-of-all-time-grand-theft-auto-minecraft-tetris.

Staples, Shelley. "The Stereoscope in America." *The Machine in the Parlor: Naturalizing and Standardizing Labor and Industry through the Stereoscope* (blog). Accessed 23 January 2023. http://xroads.virginia.edu/~MA03/staples/stereo/stereographs.html.

Stokes, Evelyn. "Te Waharoa, Wiremu Tāmihana Tarapīpipi." *Dictionary of New Zealand Biography*, first published in 1990, updated February 2006. Accessed 23 January 2023. https://teara.govt.nz/en/biographies/1t82/te-waharoa-wiremu-tamihana-tarapipipi.

"The Royal Game of Ur." Otago Museum. Accessed 23 January 2023. https://otagomuseum.nz/athome/the-royal-game-of-ur.

Thompson, Clive. "Stereographs Were the Original Virtual Reality." *Smithsonian Magazine*. October 2017. https://www.smithsonianmag.com/innovation/sterographs-original-virtual-reality-180964771.

Voorhies, Barbara. *An Archaic Mexican Shellmound and Its Entombed Floors*. Los Angeles: The Cotsen Institute of Archaeology Press, 2015.

Voorhies, Barbara. "Games Ancient People Played." *Archaeology*, 65, no. 3 (2012). https://archive.archaeology.org/1205/features/tlacuachero_chiapas_patolli_hualapai.html.

RITES AND RITUALS

Bhatia, Anchal. "The Significance of the Sacred Thread Ceremony before Marriage." Wedding Wire. 7 March 2019. https://www.weddingwire.in/wedding-tips/thread-ceremony--c2985.

Curry, Andrew. "Ancient Greeks Didn't Kill 'Weak' Babies, New Study Argues." *Science*. 10 December 2021. https://www.science.org/content/article/ancient-greeks-didn-t-kill-weak-babies-new-study-argues.

Docevski, Boban. "Walkabout – The Aboriginal Australian Hike That Serves as a Rite of Passage." Outdoor Revival. 6 April 2017. https://www.outdoorrevival.com/old-ways/walkabout-aboriginal-australian-hike-serves-rite-passage.html.

Encyclopædia Britannica, Eds. "Upanayana." In *Encyclopædia Britannica*, online edition. Accessed 23 January 2023. https://www.britannica.com/topic/upanayana.

"Initiation: The Sacred Thread Ceremony." The Heart of Hinduism, ISKCON Educational Services, UK. Accessed 23 January 2023. https://iskconeducationalservices.org/HoH/practice/rites-of-passage/initiation-the-sacred-thread-ceremony.

Milligan, Susan J. "The Treatment of Infants in Classical and Hellenistic Greece." PhD diss., University of Glasgow, 1989. Enlighten: Theses (glathesis:1989-77952).

"Saging the World: Supporting Indigenous-led efforts to safeguard white sage." California Native Plant Society. Accessed 23 January 2023. https://www.cnps.org/conservation/white-sage.

Sheets, Brian. "Papers or Plastic: the Difficulty in Protecting Native Spiritual Identity." *Lewis & Clark Law Review*, 17, no. 2 (2013): 591-635. https://law.lclark.edu/live/files/14090-lcb172art8sheetspdf.

Shizuka, Satsuki. "Guan Li, the coming-of-age ritual." *Toronto Guqin Society* (blog). 8 July 2009. https://torguqin.wordpress.com/2009/07/08/guan-li.

"Solo Shirt Cutting: An Aviation Tradition." AeroGuard Flight Training Center. 18 December 2019. https://www.flyaeroguard.com/blog/2019/12/18/solo-shirt-cutting.

"South Pentecost." Pulotu: Database of Austronesian Religions. Accessed 23 January 2023. https://pulotu.com/culture/south_pentecost.

Vanuaranu, Ari. "Ulwaluko (traditional male circumcision)." Part of the project entitled "Initiation (Ulwaluko) in South Africa." Last updated September 2015. https://www.researchgate.net/publication/306253845_Ulwaluko_traditional_male_circumcision.

Vučković, Aleksa. "Land Diving in Vanuatu: Would You Take the Leap of Faith?" Ancient Origins®. Last updated 30 December 2019. https://www.ancient-origins.net/history-ancient-traditions/land-diving-0013070.

LOVE AND SEXUALITY

Baumgart, Phillip, and Shariq Farooqi. "India's hijras find themselves further marginalized amid the pandemic." The Atlantic Council. 17 July 2020. https://www.atlanticcouncil.org/blogs/new-atlanticist/indias-hijras-find-themselves-further-marginalized-amid-the-pandemic.

Bresler, Alex. "7 Courtship Customs around the World." Matador Network. 10 February 2020. https://matadornetwork.com/read/courtship-customs-around-world.

Cox, Savannah, Ed. "The Five Most Interesting Wedding Traditions from Around the World." All That's Interesting. Last updated 6 November 2019. https://allthatsinteresting.com/interesting-wedding-traditions.

"Encyclopædia Britannica, Eds. "Dowry." In *Encyclopædia Britannica*, online edition. Accessed 23 January 2023. https://www.britannica.com/topic/dowry.

"Eskimo Identification Tags Replaced Traditional Names." Indigenous Corporate Training Inc. 16 September 2016. https://www.ictinc.ca/blog/eskimo-identification-tags-replaced-traditional-names.

"German Wedding Traditions – The Hochzeitslader, the Polterabend and the Baumstamm Sägen." Business Weddings. 14 February 2020. https://www.businessweddings.com/2020/02/14/german-wedding-traditions.

Hays, Jeff. "Yugur Minority." Facts and Details. Accessed 23 January 2023. https://factsanddetails.com/china/cat5/4sub6/entry-4350.html#chapter-7.

Hersher, Rebecca. "Why You Probably Shouldn't Say 'Eskimo'." NPR. 24 April 2016. https://www.npr.org/sections/goatsandsoda/2016/04/24/475129558/why-you-probably-shouldnt-say-eskimo.

Huntsberger, Alex. "Love and Money: A Brief History of Dowries." OppU. Last updated 18 March 2021. https://www.opploans.com/oppu/articles/love-and-money-a-brief-history-of-dowries.

Hylton, Sara. "The Peculiar Position of India's Third Gender." *The New York Times*. 17 February 2018. https://www.nytimes.com/2018/02/17/style/india-third-gender-hijras-transgender.html.

Inuit Art Foundation. "Atiq (Naming Your Soul)." *Inuit Art Quarterly*. Accessed 23 January 2023. https://www.inuitartfoundation.org/inuit-art-quarterly/special-series/naming-series.

Lal, Vinay. "Not This, Not That: The Hijras of India and the Cultural Politics of Sexuality." *Social Text*, 61, vol. 17, no. 4 (Winter 1999): 119-140. https://www.jstor.org/stable/488683.

"Native American Marriage." Native American Netroots. Accessed 23 January 2023. http://nativeamericannetroots.net/diary/1084.

Razga, Kirk. "Tabua and Whale Tooth Ornaments from Fiji." The Australian Museum. Last updated 15 April 2019. https://australian.museum/learn/cultures/pacific-collection/melanesian/tabua-whale-tooth-ornaments-fiji.

Rhude, Kristofer. "The Third Gender and Hijras." Hinduism Case Study: Gender, part of The Religious Literacy Project, edited by Diane L. Moore, Harvard University. Last updated 2018, accessed 23 January 2023. https://rpl.hds.harvard.edu/religion-context/case-studies/gender/third-gender-and-hijras.

Rogers, Sarah. "Kinship Naming among Inuit Unites Family and Community." *Nunatsiaq News*. 17 July 2014. https://nunatsiaq.com/stories/article/kinship_naming_among_inuit_unites_family_and_community.

Solomon, Serena. "In Fiji, Nothing Says 'I Love You' like a Sperm Whale Tooth." *The New York Times*. 11 April 2017. https://www.nytimes.com/2017/04/11/world/asia/suva-fiji-tabua.html.

"The Introduce of The Yugur Wedding." Made In China®. 5 December 2012. https://resources.made-in-china.com/article/culture-life/IxQJFztKTEIL/-Cupid-s-Arrows-at-the-Wedding-of-the-Yugur-Ethnic-Minority.

FASHION AND BEAUTY

Adhav, Lauren. "A History of Polka Dots, in Case You're Wondering How They Came to Be." Yahoo!Sports. 19 June 2020. https://sports.yahoo.com/history-polka-dots-case-youre-190000732.html.

Bass, Tasia. "Why Are They Called Polka Dots?" *Mental Floss*. 23 August 2021. https://www.mentalfloss.com/article/649669/polka-dots-history.

Cartwright, Mark. "Tyrian Purple." *World History Encyclopedia*. Last updated 21 July 2016. https://www.worldhistory.org/Tyrian_Purple.

"Clothing in the Ancient World." History of Clothing. Accessed 23 January 2023. http://www.historyofclothing.com/clothing-history/ancient-clothing.

"Crinolines Fashion History." Fashion-Era. Last updated 28 December 2022. https://fashion-era.com/crinolines.htm#Crinolines.

Dvorsky, George. "Why Is This 4,500 Year-Old Purse Covered with a Hundred Dog Teeth?" *Gizmodo*. 29 June 2012. https://gizmodo.com/why-is-this-4-500-year-old-purse-covered-with-a-hundred-5922328.

Elephant Mask for the Kuosi Society. Early twentieth century, glass beads and cloth. Saint Louis Art Museum. https://www.slam.org/collection/objects/52072.

Erogbogbo, Yejide. "10 Crazy Fashion Trends from History." The Culture Trip. 6 October 2016. https://theculturetrip.com/europe/france/paris/articles/10-crazy-fashion-trends-from-history.

Grovier, Kelly. "Tyrian Purple: The Disgusting Origins of the Colour Purple." *BBC Culture*, BBC. 1 August 2016. https://www.bbc.com/culture/article/20180801-tyrian-purple-the-regal-colour-taken-from-mollusc-mucus.

"KAIA Small Satchel in Raffia and Leather." Yves Saint Laurent. Accessed 23 January 2023. https://www.ysl.com/en-hr/kaia-small-satchel-in-raffia-and-leather-619740GG66W7063.html.

Klemm, Peri, and Steven Zucker. "Elephant Mask (Bamileke Peoples)." Smarthistory. 11 November 2015. https://smarthistory.org/elephant-mask-kuosi-society-bamileke-peoples-cameroon.

Lavoie, Amy. "Oldest-Known Fibers to Be Used by Humans Discovered." *Harvard Gazette*. 10 September 2009. https://news.harvard.edu/gazette/story/2009/09/oldest-known-fibers-discovered.

"Māori Tattoo: The Definitive Guide to Tā Moko." Zealand Tattoo. Accessed 23 January 2023. https://www.zealandtattoo.co.nz/tattoo-styles/maori-tattoo.

Radovčić, Davorka, et al. "Evidence for Neandertal Jewelry: Modified White-Tailed Eagle Claws at Krapina." *PLOS ONE* 10, no. 3 (March 2015). https://journals.plos.org/plosone/article?id=10.1371%2Fjournal.pone.0119802.

Rimi, Aisha. "Levi jeans from 1800s found in abandoned mine shaft sell for $87,000." *The Independent*. 13 October 2022. https://www.independent.co.uk/news/world/americas/oldest-pair-of-levi-jeans-auction-b2201880.html.

Synar, Edwyna. "Remember the Ladies: Oklahoma's First Miss America." *Muskogee Phoenix*. 22 November 2019. https://www.muskogeephoenix.com/news/remember-the-ladies-oklahomas-first-miss-america/article_d139f9f1-66da-5256-9191-81816f42a088.html.

"Tā Moko: Traditional Māori Tattoo." Tourism New Zealand. Accessed 23 January 2023. https://www.newzealand.com/int/feature/ta-moko-maori-tattoo.

"This Day in History (May 20): Levi Strauss and Jacob Davis Patent Blue Jeans." History, A&E Television Networks. Accessed 20 January 2023. https://www.history.com/this-day-in-history/levi-strauss-and-jacob-davis-receive-patent-for-blue-jeans.

"Tyrian Purple, the Colour of Royalty." Citizen Wolf. Accessed 23 January 2023. https://www.citizenwolf.com/blogs/news/tyrian-purple-the-colour-of-royalty.

Vela, Kyara. "Raffia Cloth." *Fashion History Timeline*. Last updated 20 July 2021. https://fashionhistory.fitnyc.edu/raffia-cloth.

Warren, Liz. "100-Year-Old Levi's Jeans Plucked from California Mine." *Rivet*. 17 September 2021. https://sourcingjournal.com/denim/denim-brands/levis-jeans-100-years-old-mine-cerro-gordo-california-brent-underwood-299600.

"What's All the Hoopla?" The Ultimate History Project. Accessed 23 January 2023. http://ultimatehistoryproject.com/crinoline.html.

EDUCATION AND WORK

"3,200-Year-Old Egyptian Tablet Records Excuses for Why People Missed Work: 'the Scorpion Bit Him,' 'Brewing Beer' & More." Open Culture. 17 February 2022. https://www.openculture.com/2022/02/3200-year-old-egyptian-tablet-shows-why-people-missed-work-the-scorpion-bit-him-brewing-beer-more.html.

American Friends of Tel Aviv University. "First evidence of farming in Mideast 23,000 years ago: Evidence of earliest small-scale agricultural cultivation." ScienceDaily. 22 July 2015. https://www.sciencedaily.com/releases/2015/07/150722144709.htm.

"Aztec Education: Learning at Home and School." History on the Net© 2000-2019, Salem Media. Accessed 23 January 2023. https://www.historyonthenet.com/aztec-education-at-home-and-school.

Blumberg, Naomi. "Voynich manuscript." In *Encyclopædia Britannica*, online ed., last updated 31 March 2023. https://www.britannica.com/topic/Voynich-manuscript.

BPK. "Colloquia of the *Hermeneumata Pseudodositheana*: Authentic Koine Greek Conversations from Daily Life." Koine Greek. Last updated 8 April 2020. https://www.koinegreek.com/post/the-colloquia-of-the-hermeneumata-pseudodositheana-authentic-koine-greek-conversations-from-daily-l.

Burgess, Anika. "The Strange and Grotesque Doodles in the Margins of Medieval Books." *Atlas Obscura*. 9 May 2017. https://www.atlasobscura.com/articles/medieval-marginalia-books-doodles.

Callaway, Ewen. "Neanderthals made leather-working tools like those in use today." Nature (2013). https://www.nature.com/articles/nature.2013.13542.

Chen, Ting, James Kai-sing Kung, and Chicheng Ma, "Long Live *Keju*! The Persistent Effects of China's Civil Examination System." *The Economic Journal*, 130, Issue 631 (2020): 2030-2064. https://academic.oup.com/ej/article/130/631/2030/5819954.

"Complaint Tablet to EA-Nasir - World's Oldest Complaint Letter." Joy of Museums. Accessed 23 January 2023. https://joyofmuseums.com/museums/united-kingdom-museums/london-museums/british-museum/complaint-tablet-to-ea-nasir.

Djinis, Elizabeth. "2,000-Year-Old 'Yearbook'-Like Tablet Celebrates a Group of Ancient Greek Grads." *Smithsonian Magazine*. 7 June 2022. https://www.smithsonianmag.com/smart-news/2000-year-old-yearbook-like-tablet-celebrates-group-ancient-greek-grads-180980201.

Eicher, Brian. "The Work of a Breaker Boy." *The Breaker Boys* (blog). 12 November 2014. https://thebreakerboysbrianeicher.weebly.com/the-work-of-a-breaker-boy.html.

Elsesser, Kim. "Spain May Legislate Menstruation Leave – Do Women Still Need Their Periods?" *Forbes*. Accessed 23 January 2023. https://www.forbes.com/sites/kimelsesser/2022/05/18/spain-may-legislate-menstruation-leave-do-women-still-need-their-periods/?sh=29848d0e4f8d.

Encyclopædia Britannica, Eds. "Ephebus." In *Encyclopædia Britannica*, online edition. Accessed 23 January 2023. https://www.britannica.com/topic/ephebus.

Galway Beekeepers' Association. "Skeps." Galway Beekeepers' Association (Cumann Beachairí na Gaillimhe). Accessed 23 January 2023. http://galwaybeekeepers.com/skeps.

"Imperial Examinations (Keju)." New World Encyclopedia™. Accessed 23 January 2023. https://www.newworldencyclopedia.org/entry/Imperial_Examinations_(Keju).

"Land use in agriculture by the numbers." Food and Agriculture Organization of the United Nations. 7 May 2020. https://www.fao.org/sustainability/news/detail/en/c/1274219.

McDermott, Alicia. "Ancient Egyptian Worker Took Sick Leave to Embalm His Mother." Ancient Origins®. Last updated 6 August 2022. https://www.ancient-origins.net/weird-facts/work-ancient-egypt-0017104.

Miranda, Shauneen. "A Marble Slab in Storage Turned out to Be an Ancient Greek Yearbook." NPR. Last updated 7 June 2022. https://www.npr.org/2022/06/06/1103372606/ancient-greece-yearbook-discovered.

Schoep, Mark E, et al. "Productivity Loss Due to Menstruation-Related Symptoms: A Nationwide Cross-Sectional Survey among 32 748 Women." *BMJ Open* (2019). https://bmjopen.bmj.com/content/9/6/e026186.

Sinha, Manoshi. "16 Ancient Universities of India: From 3600 Plus Years Ago." *My India My Glory* (blog). Accessed 23 January 2023. https://www.myindiamyglory.com/2019/02/14/15-ancient-universities-of-india-from-3600-plus-years-ago.

"Skep History." *Beespoke Info* (blog). 22 October 2013. http://beespoke.info/2013/10/22/skep-history.

Tablet No. 131236. c. 1750 BCE, tablet. The British Museum. https://www.britishmuseum.org/collection/object/W_1953-0411-71.

The Ohio State University. "The Boys in the Breakers." Department of History, the Ohio State University. Accessed 23 January 2023. https://ehistory.osu.edu/exhibitions/gildedage/content/breakerboys.

"Voynich Manuscript." General Collection, Beinecke Rare Book and Manuscript Library, Yale University. Accessed 6 April 2023. https://beinecke.library.yale.edu/collections/highlights/voynich-manuscript.

"Voynich Manuscript." Holy Books. Accessed 6 April 2023. https://www.holybooks.com/wp-content/uploads/Voynich-Manuscript.pdf.

Ware, Tony. "A Look at the Indus Basin Irrigation System." TWL Irrigation. 23 November 2021. https://www.twl-irrigation.com/indus-basin-irrigation-system.

Washington State Department of Labor & Industries. "The Breaker Boys." Washington State Department of Labor & Industries. 5 August 2019. https://lni.wa.gov/agency/blog/articles/the-breaker-boys.

SICKNESS AND HEALTH

Ashby, Carol. "Caulis (Cabbage Stalks and Leaves)." *Life in the Roman Empire* (blog). Accessed 23 January 2023. https://carolashby.com/caulis-cabbage-stalks-leaves.

Bower, Bruce. "North America's oldest skull surgery dates to at least 3,000 years ago." *Science News*. 31 March 2022. https://www.sciencenews.org/article/skull-surgery-oldest-north-america-forehead-brain.

Bower, Bruce. "The oldest known tattoo tools were found at an ancient Tennessee site." *Science News*. 25 May 2021. https://www.sciencenews.org/article/oldest-tattoo-tools-tennessee-native-american.

Calderone, Julia. "Christopher Columbus brought a host of terrible new diseases to the New World." *Business Insider*. 12 October 2015. https://www.businessinsider.com/diseases-columbus-brought-to-americas-2015-10.

Cassidy, Lara M., et al. "A dynastic elite in monumental Neolithic society." *Nature* 582 (2020): 384-388. https://www.nature.com/articles/s41586-020-2378-6.

Curry, Andrew. "Ancient Bones Offer Clues to How Long-Ago Humans Cared for the Vulnerable." NPR. 17 June 2020. https://www.npr.org/sections/goatsandsoda/2020/06/17/878896381/ancient-bones-offer-clues-to-how-long-ago-humans-cared-for-the-vulnerable.

Fraga, Kaleena. "Inside the Tangled History of Colonists Giving Smallpox Blankets to Indigenous Americans." All That's Interesting. 26 July 2022. https://allthatsinteresting.com/smallpox-blankets.

Grün, Rainer, in *Encyclopedia of Archaeology (2008)*. "Electron Spin Resonance Dating." *Encyclopedia of Geology*, 2nd ed. Amsterdam: Elsevier, 2008. Accessed online at ScienceDirect. https://www.sciencedirect.com/topics/earth-and-planetary-sciences/electron-spin-resonance-dating.

Handwerk, Brian. "Earliest Known Amputation Was Performed in Borneo 31,000 Years Ago." *Smithsonian Magazine*. 7 September 2022. https://www.smithsonianmag.com/science-nature/earliest-known-amputation-was-performed-in-borneo-31000-years-ago-180980710.

Hao, Jason Jishun, and Michele Mittelman. "Acupuncture: Past, Present, and Future." *Global Advances in Health and Medicine* 3, no. 4 (2014): 6-8. https://www.ncbi.nlm.nih.gov/pmc/articles/PMC4104560.

"History of measles vaccination." World Health Organization (WHO). Accessed 23 January 2023. https://www.who.int/news-room/spotlight/history-of-vaccination/history-of-measles-vaccination.

Kiger, Patrick J. "Did Colonists Give Infected Blankets to Native Americans as Biological Warfare?" History, A&E Television Networks. Last updated 25 November 2019. https://www.history.com/news/colonists-native-americans-smallpox-blankets.

Klein, Christopher. "8 Fascinating Facts about Ancient Roman Medicine." History, A&E Television Networks. 12 August 2022. https://www.history.com/news/ancient-roman-medicine-galen.

Mabry, Makenzie E. "The Evolutionary History of Wild, Domesticated, and Feral *Brassica oleracea* (Brassicaceae)." *Molecular Biology and Evolution*, Vol. 38, Issue 10 (2021): 4419-4434. https://academic.oup.com/mbe/article/38/10/4419/6304875.

Mandal, Ananya. "Acupuncture History." *News Medical*. Last updated 19 June 2019. https://www.news-medical.net/health/Acupuncture-History.aspx.

"Measles." *Encyclopedia of Arkansas*, part of Central Arkansas Library System. Last updated 31 August 2022. https://encyclopediaofarkansas.net/entries/measles-5313.

"Measles History." Centers for Disease Control and Prevention. Last reviewed 5 November 2020. https://www.cdc.gov/measles/about/history.html.

Price, Michael. "World's oldest amputation: Foot removed 31,000 years ago – without modern antibiotics or painkillers." *Science*. 7 September 2022. https://www.science.org/content/article/world-s-oldest-amputation-foot-removed-31-000-years-ago-without-modern-antibiotics-or.

The Planet D. "Poulnabrone Dolmen: The Eerie Marvel of Ireland's Biggest Portal Tomb." *The Planet D* (blog). Last updated 15 January 2023. https://theplanetd.com/poulnabrone-dolmen-ireland.

White, A., and E. Ernst. "A brief history of acupuncture." *Rheumatology*, Vol. 43, Issue 5 (2004): 662-663. https://academic.oup.com/rheumatology/article/43/5/662/1788282.

Wills, Matthew. "How Commonly Was Smallpox Used as a Biological Weapon?" JSTOR Daily. 4 April 2021. https://daily.jstor.org/how-commonly-was-smallpox-used-as-a-biological-weapon.

MEMENTO MORI

"Balinese Cremation (Ngaben)." Bali. Accessed 23 January 2023. https://bali.com/bali/travel-guide/culture/balinese-cremation-ngaben.

Bonetti, Roberta. "The Media-action of *abebu adekai* (Ghana's Sculptural Coffins) in the World Market and Design: The Case of Eric Adjetey Anang." *Cahiers d'Études Africaines*, 56, no. 223 (2016): 479-502. http://www.jstor.org/stable/24758137.

"Discovery of Oldest Northern North American Human Remains Provides New Insights into Ice-Age Culture." National Science Foundation (NSF). 24 February 2011. https://www.nsf.gov/news/news_summ.jsp?cntn_id=118744.

Emery, Kate Meyers. "Upright Burial: A Mesolithic and Modern Phenomenon?" *Bones Don't Lie* (blog). 17 February 2016. https://bonesdontlie.wordpress.com/2016/02/17/upright-burial-a-mesolithic-and-modern-phenomenon.

Esser, Jessica B. "10 Unusual Ancient Burials." Listverse. 21 July 2018. https://listverse.com/2018/07/21/10-unusual-ancient-burials.

Fitzpatrick, Colette. "Mantua's Eternal Lovers - The Lovers of Valdaro." Italy Villas. 14 July 2016. https://www.italy-villas.com/to-italy/2016/curiosities/lovers-of-valdaro.

Gannon, Megan. "Interlocked Spiral of Ancient Skeletons Unearthed in Mexico City." LiveScience. 2 February 2018. https://www.livescience.com/61622-spiral-ancient-skeletons-mexico-city.html.

May, Kate Torgovnick. "Death is not the end: Fascinating funeral traditions from around the globe." TED. 1 October 2013. https://ideas.ted.com/11-fascinating-funeral-traditions-from-around-the-globe.

Mkandawire, Vinjeru. "Ghana's Fantasy Coffins." OkayAfrica. Accessed 23 January 2023. https://www.okayafrica.com/video-ghanas-fantasy-coffins.

Munnik, Jo, and Kathy Scott. "In Famadihana, Madagascar, a sacred ritual unearths the dead." Cable News Network (CNN). Last updated 27 March 2017. https://www.cnn.com/2016/10/18/travel/madagascar-turning-bones/index.html.

Putri, Edira. "A Festive Cremation: Bali's Ngaben and the Celebration of Death." The Culture Trip. 6 February 2018. https://theculturetrip.com/asia/indonesia/articles/a-festive-cremation-balis-ngaben-and-the-celebration-of-death.

Ratsara, Domoina. "Famadihana: Madagascar's Day of the Dead." The Culture Trip. 27 July 2018. https://theculturetrip.com/africa/madagascar/articles/famadihana-madagascars-day-of-the-dead.

Sullivan, Kerry. "Children of the Upward Sun River: 11,500-Year-Old Remains Shed Light on Alaska's Earliest Inhabitants." Ancient Origins®. 11 December 2016. https://www.ancient-origins.net/ancient-places-americas/children-upward-sun-river-11500-year-old-remains-shed-light-alaska-s-021109.

Terberger, Thomas, et al. "Standing upright to all eternity – The Mesolithic Burial Site at Groß Fredenwalde, Brandenburg (NE Germany)." *Quartär. International Yearbook for Ice Age and Stone Age Research.* 62 (2015): 133-153. https://journals.ub.uni-heidelberg.de/index.php/qu/article/view/78405.

"The Birthplace of a Tradition." Kane Kwei Carpentry Workshop. Accessed 23 January 2023. http://www.kanekwei.com/about.

Urbanus, Jason. "Eternal Embrace." *Archaeology*, 61, no. 1 (2008). https://archive.archaeology.org/0801/abstracts/valdaro.html.

Webb, Sara. "Bali Celebrates Biggest Royal Cremation in Decades." Reuters. Accessed 23 January 2023. https://www.reuters.com/article/bali-cremation/bali-celebrates-biggest-royal-cremation-in-decades-idUKORM53901320080715.

Weiner, Sophie. "Scientists Are Stumped by This Mysterious Spiral of Ancient Skeletons." *Popular Mechanics.* 2 February 2018. https://www.popularmechanics.com/science/archaeology/a16259553/scientists-are-stumped-by-this-mysterious-spiral-of-ancient-skeletons.

INDEX

THE ENCYCLOPEDIA OF THE WEIRD AND WONDERFUL

THE ENCYCLOPEDIA OF THE WEIRD AND WONDERFUL

ACKNOWLEDGMENTS

There are several people without whose help this book would never have been possible. I'd like to take a moment here to personally thank them for making this book a reality.

First and foremost, I'd like to thank Elizabeth You for being my guide through the weird and wonderful world of writing a manuscript. Our weekly meetings helped me refine this book from an unguided concept to the product you see before you today. If it weren't for her, the book before you today either wouldn't exist or would just be a complete trainwreck.

I would also like to extend a huge thank you to Molly Morrison, whose research prowess helped inform the "Love and Sexuality" chapter as well as further research in "Rites and Rituals." Her expertise in these fields was invaluable in shaping these chapters to the state they are in before you.

And for giving me the ability to write these words today I want to also thank Katie Moore, who reached out to me initially to gauge my interest in undertaking this project. While our work together was only confined to the first couple weeks of writing, without her this project would never have even begun.

Beyond those who helped with the book, there are a couple others who deserve a thank you for helping keep my other operations running while I worked on this project.

I'd like to extend a massive thank you to Gianfranco Botto, for helping me keep my videos rolling out as I worked to complete this project. I would have been fully incapable of juggling both YouTube and writing had it not been for his editorial skills and dedicated work.